William Newton

Twenty Years on the Saskatchewan, N. W. Canada

William Newton

Twenty Years on the Saskatchewan, N. W. Canada

ISBN/EAN: 9783337190439

Printed in Europe, USA, Canada, Australia, Japan

Cover: Foto ©ninafisch / pixelio.de

More available books at **www.hansebooks.com**

CANON NEWTON.

TWENTY YEARS

ON THE

SASKATCHEWAN,

N. W. CANADA.

BY THE

REV. WILLIAM NEWTON,

HON. CANON OF SASKATCHEWAN.

LONDON:

ELLIOT STOCK, 62, PATERNOSTER ROW, E.C.

1897.

PREFACE.

THIS book contains a narrative of the life and thoughts of a simple missionary during twenty years spent in North-Western Canada. It is dedicated, with much respect, to those dear friends on both sides of the sea who have so often cheered this missionary with their help and sympathy.

To make the experience of the missionary appear real to other people, it has been necessary to speak of many personal and local matters; but the general subjects that are mentioned will have their interest for readers whose thoughts may be turning sometimes to North-Western Canada, and especially to the Edmonton district of Alberta, as this has been the centre of the missionary work that is narrated, and the standpoint of the observations that are made on the history, races, and customs of the people brought under review.

The references that are made to the origin of our Indian tribes, and their intimate relationship with Eastern Asia, only represent a small part of the results of the missionary's reading and reflection on the whole problem of ancient America. Of the correctness of the views that are given as to the substantial identity of the languages and peoples of America and Asia, there is little room for doubt. To those learned authors who take a different view of the origin of the North American Indians, I can only plead, that circumstances have helped me to a conclusion which I might never have reached, had I not lived so long on the border-lands of the far West. But before residing here I had given some attention to the customs, ideas, and languages of the far East.

It also gives me great pleasure to note that the public at home are turning their attention to this part of the world as one of its ancient centres, where events are transpiring that are likely to affect the destiny of England and the British Empire.

The present writer may live to visit Europe by travelling over the Siberian Railway, the opening of which will be a new epoch in the world's history. Japan may checkmate Russia in the North Pacific. And if Japan or Russia should marshal the yellow races, what will come after to Europe, and even to America? Solitary students even in the far-off wildernesses are dreaming of these things, and their anxious hope is that England will be prepared for the changes which are even now at hand.

I have only to add that a portion of the chapter which gives an account of the Right Reverend John McLean, the first Bishop of Saskatchewan, was written by his widow, and it will, no doubt, be read with the respect which it deserves.

CONTENTS.

LIST OF ILLUSTRATIONS.

Page 34, line 14 from top, read '*might* have been secured.'

,, 54, ,, 8 ,, read '*and* her brother was a Japanese.'

clergymen to serve as missionaries. As a result of his appeal, it was arranged that I should go to Edmonton as the missionary supported by the Society for the Propagation of the Gospel.

During the winter before my journey, I had time to look about me, and to make inquiries concerning the countries which I purposed to visit, and concerning the best means of getting to them. A Methodist missionary from the Saskatchewan visited

I

CHAPTER I.

I N the spring of 1875 I left my parish in the Toronto diocese to become a missionary in 'the far North-West.' Little at that time was known of this great district by the people of Canada, and my undertaking was a sufficiently serious one, in consideration of the means that were placed at my disposal. In the summer of 1874 the first Bishop of Saskatchewan had been consecrated at Lambeth. On his return to his diocese he had met the provincial synod of the Church of England in session at Montreal, and had appealed for two clergymen to serve as missionaries. As a result of his appeal, it was arranged that I should go to Edmonton as the missionary supported by the Society for the Propagation of the Gospel.

During the winter before my journey, I had time to look about me, and to make inquiries concerning the countries which I purposed to visit, and concerning the best means of getting to them. A Methodist missionary from the Saskatchewan visited

1

Ontario during that winter, and made speeches which were reported in the newspapers; but I could gather very little from them that was of practical service to me. A large map, which had been published by the General Government of Canada gave me some idea of the Hudson Bay trading-posts, and of the vast distances between them; but, evidently to cover ignorance, the intervening spaces were dotted with the names of Indian tribes who did—or at least were supposed to—roam somewhere between those posts.

It looked a very serious business to get to Edmonton and the mountain district around it, without any well-defined means of transit. I should have to journey through a region where there were no public boats, no bridges crossing the rivers, no guides whom I could hire, and no means of protection either from rude white men or from savage Indians. So matters seemed to a simple clergyman, who had undertaken the work of the Church, in obedience to the call of Divine Providence. The way was by no means plain, but it was the way of faith, and with God for Guide and Protector, surely even more uncertain and perilous journeys might be hopefully undertaken.

On arriving at Collingwood, on the south point of the Georgian Bay, with a favourite horse, a light buckboard, and an English orphan boy as my servant and companion, I found the ice was still in the bay, but the vessel ready to proceed as soon as practicable up the Great Lakes. I had a day or two of pleasant waiting at the hospitable Rectory, and then the generous Rector, Dr. Lett, did me a last kindness, and gave me his last farewell.

The way up the Great Lakes, even in those days, was a well-travelled route as far as Prince Arthur's Landing. This place was named after one of the Queen's sons, who had gone up as far as this, in his Canadian travels, in order to see something of the fine scenery of the lakes. At the time of the Prince's visit the place was a mere cedar swamp, at one corner of a noble bay of water, near to Fort William; but now it is a splendid town, and of great promise for the future.

The boat by which we travelled arrived at Prince Arthur's Landing late on the Saturday night, or, rather, early on the Sunday morning, and, as it was the first boat of the season, all the people from far and near gathered together to meet her, and the little place was crowded with quite a mass of people. No place—not even a bed on the floor—could be obtained at any hotel; and though we searched everywhere, we could hear of no shelter in any building. So, although it was the Sunday morning, we had to purchase a tent, and pitch it on the shore of the bay, to buy food for the horse, and to make ourselves as comfortable as we could under the circumstances. At eleven o'clock we went to the little church, and assisted the clergyman in reading prayers. At the evening service we were invited to preach the sermon.

Now commenced the rough part of our journey. It had been represented to us in Ontario that we

should find the new Dawson Route a very convenient and expeditious road; and as it was declared to be the direct route, and also under Government management, we were very hopeful of good
experiences. Several times, however, the road was
stated to be ready for us, and then, on presenting
ourselves to begin our journey, we were requested to
delay for a day, and then for the next day. The
truth was that the road was *not* ready, and when we
did proceed we found confusion everywhere: there
was no expedition in the transit boats on the innumerable lakes; servants were rough and unfitted
for their duties; paths or roads were ill-made, or else
not made at all, and over these we had to pass with
our goods as best we could. Everything we had,
even the buckboard, had to be taken to pieces and
put together again several times each day. Our
goods were so carelessly thrown into the light boats
that we wondered to find that our losses were so
few, and our consequent discomfort so small. Most
of our fellow-passengers were Canadian backwoods-
men, who were proceeding to Manitoba with their
teams of horses or oxen, to try their fortune on the
prairies.

Just then several parties of Government surveyors
were going out into these wilds to follow their profession, and I found them very courteous and helpful, and on several occasions I should have been in
perilous straits but for their kindly assistance. One
gentleman from Ottawa, a great big-hearted fellow,
perhaps to tease me as much as anything else,

pretended to be an outrageous sceptic. Yet he willingly allowed daily prayers in his tent, helped to get me a room for Sunday service whenever it was practicable, and generally acted so much like a good Samaritan to the missionary, that the impression still remains with me that such a man could not be far from the kingdom of God.

This Dawson Route was a long one, and the journey through it was a wearisome business; yet, like all disagreeable experiences, it came to an end at last. After the boating was done we put our buckboard together, and tried to push on ahead of the other passengers, who were more heavily laden. We had covered about thirty miles, and had arrived near a place called Oak Point, when, while we were drinking our tea, we missed our horse, and found he had been so tormented by the flies that he had broken his line and gone back again. We passed a weary and anxious night in our tent, as we were quite unable to help ourselves; but next day our fellow-passengers brought the horse along with them, and then we pressed on for Winnipeg.

On bidding farewell to this Dawson Route—up which General Wolseley came with his troops to quell the Red River rebellion—we may observe that the scenery was often very fine, and sometimes even splendid. The Nepigon and Rainey Rivers greatly impressed us with their scenes of exquisite beauty, and the passage of the falls on the latter river was an experience that would be well worth recording.

CHAPTER II.

A T the end of the month of May the prairies around Winnipeg are a sight to see. The earth is a carpet of living green, sweetly woven with golden and other colours. Nature does not appear in a gaudy dress; the fashion she wears is that of chaste simplicity, as if she did not need too much adornment. The sky overhead speaks of distance—of expansiveness; and when the true poet of the prairies shall appear, the clear blue skies of Manitoba will furnish him with many symbols of beautiful thoughts and truths.

Our first impressions of Winnipeg were not delightful ones. It was the time of the locust plague. The chief street seemed to have its full share of grog-shops. Some of the traders evidently thought the new-comers were very green, and several of the most prominent citizens proved 'quite smart' in their business transactions. Two horses which I purchased for my distant journey proved to be utterly useless creatures, and they had to be abandoned on the plains when it was very difficult to manage without them. Till I could start on my journey, of nearly a thousand miles, I lived in my tent near the old Hudson Bay Fort Garry, and I bought my experience dearly. My own idea was to start for Edmonton with two horses, and provisions enough to keep me from post to post as I went along. I proposed to travel some forty or fifty miles each day. This, however, was not considered to be the right course for me to pursue. Besides the buckboard, it was thought necessary for me to have a Red River cart and abundance of provisions, for I was told that I might not be able to procure any when I arrived at Edmonton, and the winter would be at hand. At last, in the week succeeding the sixth Sunday after Trinity, I resumed my journey from Winnipeg to Edmonton, finding the trails as I could, and meeting with all kinds of mishaps from day to day. Sometimes the horses strayed, or the Red River cart, which was built all of wood, would break down, or from careless driving or restive horses would be upset. Now and then the hills were too steep for our horses to draw up the loads, and we had to wait for assistance from some chance passers-by, who would sometimes tie the load to the horse's tail, without any harness, and so pull the load up the hill in the most absurd, yet most effective, manner.

This slow travelling on the plains becomes in time rather wearisome. You rise with the sun, take your breakfast, collect the horses, pack your tent, bedding,

and camp utensils, and start off for a ten miles
' spell.' You have no idea of what may be before
you—what creeks, or small rivers, or boggy places
you may have to encounter. All you know is, that
somehow you must be prepared to meet any difficulty and to overcome it. The worse the trouble,
the greater is the need of calm self-possession in
order that you may be able to devise some proper
expedients for meeting the new difficulty. A
freighter of course knows the road, and is accustomed to his business, and he secures the necessary
assistance; but the inexperienced clergyman has no
advantages, and finds it ' a hard road to travel ' on
his own account.

The first spell of the day done, the horses are
unharnessed and let loose to graze, wood is
collected, the kettle is boiled, the tea is made, and
the cloth is laid for dinner. An hour passes, and
then the journey is resumed as before until the
setting of the sun tells you that it is time to camp
for the night. Then you look out for good grass for
the horses, and for good wood and water. You pitch
your tent, provide your supper, and eat it heartily;
put the logs on the camp-fire, either to bake your
bread for the morrow, or to drive away the mosquitoes, or to scare the wolves from the provisions.
In the deep silence the sound of the horses' bells is
very welcome, for you know the horses have found
their pasture-ground for the night, and that they will
be easily captured in the morning. If the night is
stormy, you secure your tent-pegs and ropes; or if

the evening is calm and fine, you open the folds of the tent, and watch the changing shadows of the firelight, or you turn your eyes to the heavens, which are aglow with brilliant stars, and in the silence and the solitude you think and feel as you cannot do amid the smoke and din of great cities. To the mere traveller all this is a pleasant experience, for he knows that it is but for a little while, and he hopes to see the face of friends again, and enjoy the pleasures of reunion. But the missionary who faces the silence and the solitude knows not how long a time his separation may last; his worldly hopes are but few; he has no lust of gold like the miner; he is not in quest of new discoveries, as is the scientific traveller, nor is commerce his aim, in common with the trader or the merchant. His hope in his exile is to be able to build folds for the Good Shepherd, and to gather souls therein who have been redeemed, and need to be prepared for everlasting blessedness. In new lands the missionary desires to plant those seeds of Christian civilization which will grow up to regenerate the nations when he is dead and gone. Bright are the visions of usefulness which God permits the missionary to see in his times of solitude and exile. The Christian missionary asks for no pity; for if the Christian religion be true, his is the most noble work on which the sun looks down.

Before we reached Fort Carlton we met with an accident which might have had serious results. A mare which we had been obliged to purchase on the road was really too young for her work of drawing the Red River cart, and I had often asked the man whom I engaged to drive her to get down and walk up the hills, to make her load more easy, and to give her a fair chance of getting safely to Edmonton. The man was often too indolent to do this, and on coming to steep places he would sit upright, and allow himself to be drawn with great dignity up the hills. He was an old Scotch soldier, and had several medals for brave deeds done in the Indian Mutiny, and he served us out of pure condescension. Thinking it as well to let this gentleman use the buckboard, and for me, as the master, to take a humble place, I gave up the buckboard to him, and mounted the Red River cart, intending to teach him, by my example, how to walk up hills and lighten the mare's burden. On coming to the hills I did this once or twice successfully, but the Red River cart is an awkward vehicle to get up on and down from, and some tent-poles with long spikes projected close by the shaft near which I had to descend to the ground. As fate would have it, on coming to the next hill, when alighting I in some way frightened the mare, so that she began to kick, and then gallop at a furious rate. I was all the while sitting on the shaft of the cart, and expecting every moment that the heels of the mare would dash my head on to the spikes of the tent-poles close by me. Looking back in my danger, I could see the man of many medals as calm as usual, and much too full of dignity to exercise the courage and quick-wittedness which may have won him distinction on the far plains of

India. Of course the events in India were great ones, and he was equal to *such* occasions; but this Red River cart business was beneath contempt, and not at all worth the risk of personal harm, when no distinction could possibly be won from an admiring country. What, then, was I to do? for the danger seemed to be imminent, and there was no time to be lost. My feet were hanging from the shaft, and I could only spring from the elbows, and I could not hope to do that far enough to avoid the risk of breaking both my legs by the passage over them of the eight or nine hundred pounds weight of goods which the cart contained. Instead, therefore, of springing too far, I quietly dropped under the wheel just where the weight would pass over the strong thigh-bones with the chance of not breaking them. The plan answered very well, but of course the shock was great to the whole system, so that I swooned away. Recovering consciousness, I was placed in the buck-board, and then tried to travel on a few miles; but the pain compelled me to have the tent pitched, and as the next day was the Sunday, we rested in a most desolate place, but I was quietly grateful that, in God's mercy, things had turned out no worse.

At Fort Carlton we remained for three weeks, and received many kindnesses from the gentlemen in charge. Up to this time we had met very few Indians, and they had not molested us in any way. Now and then a brave had ridden up to us with his gun cocked, half begging and half demanding tŏbāccō, but that was all the annoyance we had

suffered ; as we proceeded, however, we found the
Indians discontented and restless, and adverse to
the passage of white men through their territories.
Before we reached the farther plains we learned
that a party of surveyors had been forced to return,
and that the Indians had proclaimed their intention
of stopping all strangers. In our little party at this
time we had a trader going west, and two Chippewa
Indians with their families. The presence of these
Indians was a source of danger to us, for the
Chippewas were hunters, and as these men had
killed some buffaloes during their journey they were
sure to be discovered. The Crees considered that
no strangers ought to kill their game, especially as
it was exceedingly scarce, and their families were
often in want. We were not surprised, therefore,
when, one Saturday evening, just south of Fort Pitt,
in the delta of the Saskatchewans, an Indian and a
boy presented themselves in our encampment, and,
after observing everything, told us that they had
been sent by their band to learn who we were, and
to order us to return eastward, for they were
determined not to allow us to proceed through their
country. On receiving this message, we invited the
two Indians to share our supper, and requested
them to wait while I prepared a communication
which they could deliver to their chief and people.
In this letter I told the chief, in very respectful
language, who we were, and that the great chiefs of
the English Church had sent me to teach the people
around Edmonton the way of the true Christian

religion, and that of course I must go on my journey, and do the work which I had been sent to do. I said I hoped that I should be able to see him and his people on Monday, and that so we might become friends and brothers together, which would give me great satisfaction.

During the Sunday, and on the Monday morning, I noticed the people in our encampment were often in conference together, and that they were anxious about the state of matters; and when we started on the trail I observed that they soon left it, and did not return to it. When I inquired the reason of their leaving the trail, they answered that they wished to find a good crossing of the Battle River, as the usual crossing was a difficult one. However, no crossing could be found, and, on turning a bend in the stream, behold the whole plain was covered with tents, and there were the very Indians that our people had secretly desired to avoid. The trader and the Chippewas looked confounded, and would have escaped if they could have done so. They would thus have brought themselves into danger, for on the plains the Indians seem to observe everything, and fear and flight will never secure protection from them. However, all this turned out well in the end, for the Indians were invited to hold a conference, and when they were seated in circles around the spot reserved for the missionary, he appeared in a formal manner, arrayed in all possible finery, and first gravely distributed plugs of tobacco to all who were seated in the nearest circles.

Then, inquiring whether they were all ready for the conference, he wished to know whether they had received the letter which he had sent. They had, they said. Then he explained again who he was, and what he was sent to do, and asked whether the message to order such a man to go back was reasonable. They answered that it was not. Then, should we be friends and brothers, and would they assist me on the journey, for I was a stranger in their land? They would give me all the help and furtherance they were able, they replied. So with many expressions of good feeling we departed, and for two hundred miles we found the Indians friendly everywhere. This good feeling has been maintained during the vicissitudes of twenty long years.

A short time after this another Cree appeared, and this also was on a Saturday evening. He inquired whether I would go twenty miles to his encampment, and hold a service with his people. If so, he would take me there, and send me back to the trail after the service. Who he was I knew not, nor where he wished to take me. However, I went, and found perhaps twenty tents beside a small lake, and saw for the first and last time a great herd of buffaloes close by the encampment. This man proved to be the chief of the White Fish Lake Indians, and one of Nature's noblemen.

Our trail ran nearly west from Carlton to the Battle River; then, turning northward, we made for Buffalo Lake, and for the trail which leads from the Bow River to Edmonton. The scenery about here was charming, and I never conceived it to be possible for so many fowls to be collected together as I saw around Buffalo Lake in that September. Water and air seemed alive with them, and you could not fire a gun without bringing down several with every shot. The fecundity of Nature, when she is left alone in these regions, is marvellous.

Fort Edmonton came in sight on September 28, 1875. The journey from Ontario took five months. Now, in the year 1896, it is possible in that period to visit the British Isles from Edmonton several times with far less toil and inconvenience than I had to endure in that single journey twenty years ago.

CHAPTER III.

EARLY DIFFICULTIES.

E DMONTON, Alberta, North-West Canada, is
at the head of navigation on the North Saskatchewan River, which flows through Lake Winnipeg into Hudson Bay. Twenty years ago it was
simply a fort, where hunters brought their furs,
and received goods in exchange. On my arrival I
found very few residents, and these were nearly all
servants of the Hudson Bay Company. Nine miles
from the fort were the headquarters of the Roman
Catholic Church, and the Catholics had, at that
time, a church inside the fort itself. Within sight
of the fort were also a Methodist chapel and a
parsonage. The leading people at the fort were
Methodists, and very zealous Methodists too. They
did not often attend our services, nor did they
encourage their servants to attend. At first, on
looking around me, I asked myself what I was to
do. I was far from civilization, and with only one
or two posts in the year to bring me letters. I had
at hand a tent, a surplice, a Prayer-Book, and a

Bible. There was no parsonage, no church, nor any means for building either. I had been sent as a missionary to settlers. But where were they? I could not find such persons as we usually designate settlers. Beyond the mission-stations even a potato-patch was seldom to be seen, and a farm never.

VIEW OF EDMONTON.

Three or four persons had, in years gone by, been confirmed in the church at Manitoba, but these had become attendants on Methodist ministrations. It seemed as if I had come to upset Methodism, and to introduce religious strife into a distant, and not very devout, community. I would gladly have re-

2

turned to other fields of labour, could I have been so directed, or had circumstances permitted. Then as to my means of subsistence. Two hundred pounds a year in Edmonton was equal to about fifty pounds a year in Ontario or in England. The usual price of flour was twenty-five dollars a bag, or five pounds sterling the hundredweight. Fifty cents, or two shillings, bought a pound of sugar or of salt. During the first two winters I bought barley for my mare, and it cost me one pound sterling for two bushels. If the mare strayed away—and this she often did—then to fetch her from the plains cost me five dollars a day, or part of a day, as the case might be; but if the business took two days, a man expected two sovereigns as his pay. All my expenses were in the same proportion.

For a few days I received kindly hospitality at the fort, and then I removed into a log building, which was partly finished, and available by a mere accident. I used this both as a residence and as the church. As the winter was at hand, it was necessary for me to put this house into some sort of repair, and the difficulty I had was to secure both lumber and a carpenter. After some inquiry, I found a man who had recently arrived from Manitoba with his family, and I learned that he might be induced to do the job for me. The man was sent for.

' Can you do this job ?' I asked.

' Well, I might,' he replied, ' if the pay is all right.'

' What do you want a day for this work ?' I said.

' Well, I'll ax around, and see; it may be five dollars a day might pay me,' was the answer.

The man did not look a very active carpenter, but the work had to be done, and so I said :

' All right, you shall have five dollars a day; come to-morrow.'

Days passed, however, and no carpenter appeared. After awhile a large tent was pitched at a little distance from the house, and it was crowded with boys and girls of all ages; there were ten of them, and the carpenter was among them. Thinking, and hoping, that he had come to begin the work at last, I approached him with the question :

' Have you come to fix the house ?'

' No,' he said, ' I think not ; the pay is not enough.'

' What do you want, then ?' was the answer.

' Oh, food for my family, and five dollars a day.'

' What ! food for all these ?'

' Yes.'

' How much will the food cost ?'

' I do not know, but I must have food for my family.'

' Well, then, buy it out of the five dollars.'

' No, I can't ; they want that in other ways.'

I need hardly say that this carpenter was not engaged on these impossible conditions.

The first winter I spent at Edmonton was a very cold and severe one, the frost often registering forty, and even fifty, degrees below zero. I was fortunate enough to obtain a small cooking stove at the fort, which, with the pipes, cost one hundred dollars, or twenty pounds sterling. This stove was not sufficient to warm the room, and it needed perpetual attention night and day, with the slight wood of the country, to keep us from freezing in our badly-built house. Often I tried to write, and placed the ink on the front of the stove in order that it might thaw; but before the pen could touch the paper and write a word the ink in the pen would be frozen, and writing exceedingly difficult. At this time my books had not arrived, and there was very little literature to be obtained. The days were short and the nights were long, so if there had been at command a large library, the books would have been of no practical use, for, besides the cold, we had no light, and could not procure any. Neither coal nor oil could be bought, and tallow for making candles cost fifty cents a pound, and only about two pounds could be purchased during the winter even at this price. To help in bearing the cold, I ordered a jacket of moose-skin and a pair of trousers. The charge was fifty dollars, and I actually paid forty-five. Some of these charges I have since compared with the charges made by traders for the necessaries of life up among the great newly-discovered lakes in Central Africa, such as Lakes Tanganyika and Victoria Nyanza, and it is a positive fact that we, in North-West America, then paid more for common goods than the missionaries did in the far African regions.

The reader may well imagine that life under such conditions of exile and solitude would not be considered a delightful state of human existence anywhere; and yet even here the dark cloud had its silver lining. From the first a few persons attended the services. Officials in the Hudson Bay Company's service were glad to renew old church associations as they passed to other forts. Camps of surveyors sought a little Sunday rest, and change from the monotony of their life on the prairies, in public worship after the manner of their fathers. Mounted police, who had just come into the country, and were located some eighteen or twenty miles away, were offered frequent services. Children were collected for instruction; the Indian tents were visited; and the banner of the Church was unfurled over a new, and vast, and hitherto unoccupied region.

Such occupations and thoughts made 'life worth living,' and I am thankful that the honour fell on me of being the pioneer missionary of what is now an extensive diocese.

CHAPTER IV.

DOG-TRAIN EXPERIENCES.

DURING the winter of 1875, and the summer of 1876, the monotony of the missionary's life was broken by the occurrence of a few incidents. In such circumstances as I was then placed in, small things may seem to become very large. Few events can happen in so isolated a place as Edmonton then was, and when incidents do occur, they are sure to get fixed on the memory. The Chief Factor of the Hudson Bay Fort spent this particular winter in the district. He would often pay me a visit, and even sometimes would come to dinner. Our usual food was pemmican, but on these special occasions we managed a little soup, or even went to the luxury of a pudding. The ingredients of these luxuries were of various kinds, and the cooking results were not always the same. But we expected little, and were more than satisfied if the dinner proved to be presentable. After dinner would come such conversations and confidences as can only be born out of the intimacies of times of solitude.

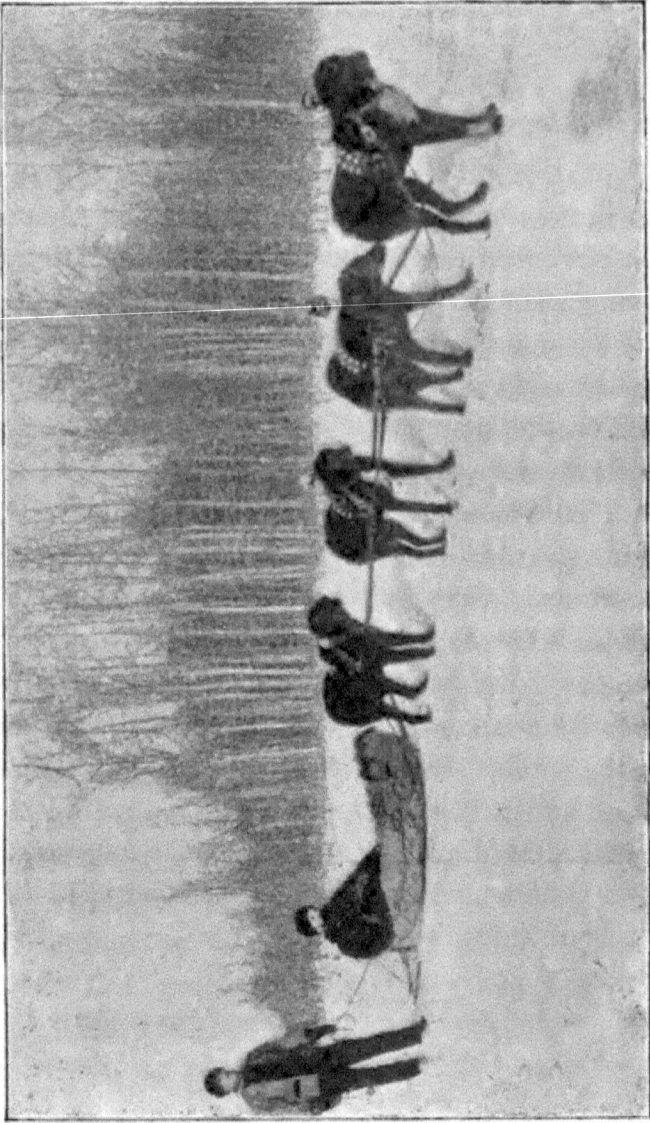

A DOG-TRAIN.

This winter, too, the surveyors were at work surveying for the Canada Pacific Railway through the passes of the Rocky Mountains, and they made their head-quarters at Edmonton. Now and then they came in, with their dog-trains, to do business, and then would take me back with them twenty, thirty, forty, and sometimes even fifty, miles on the survey line. On these occasions I was glad to hold services with the men; or on a week-night, after they had returned from their work, and finished their supper, to give them a lecture on some subject in which they were likely to be interested. These visits were often very pleasant to me, and I hope they were also helpful to the men who were in the camps that I visited.

At these camps there would be perhaps fifty persons, forming a company of the most varied kind, gathered from every part of the Dominion and of the British Isles. Their work was much the same from day to day, whether it was cold or warm, or whether it was wet or dry, and they found it exceedingly monotonous. Hence, a fresh face and a voice of kindness were always very welcome in the camp, and served to remind them of the world they had left so far away.

The gentlemen who led these camps were often very clever in their profession, and their manners were agreeable and refined, entitling them to much respect. When railroads are finished, and travellers are using them for comfortable and expeditious journeys, how little men think of the labour, and enterprise, and endurance of some of the best sons of Canada in doing the necessary pioneer work!

It was at this time that I had my first experience of travelling by a dog-train. You are wrapped up like a mummy, and placed in the cariole; a man stands or runs behind you and drives the dogs; you are perfectly quiet, and have nothing to do, either uphill, downhill, or on level ground, except to observe the dogs, the driver, and the scenery, and you are taken out at sunset, after having done your fifty or sixty miles, with very little either of discomfort or of weariness.

At the time I am writing there are very few dog-trains seen in this district; they have had their day, and are passing away, leaving the wise man to think of the compensations that attend upon all changed earthly conditions.

About this time I paid my first visit to the St. Albert Roman Catholic Mission, which was nine miles from the fort. It had been intimated to me that the Bishop's nephew was to be received into the priesthood, and that, if I would go and see the function, and take luncheon with the Bishop, it would be received as an act of politeness, and I could make acquaintance with the Roman clergy who would be gathered together on this occasion. I found a convenient church for such a far-off mission, and the service was rendered as in the front parts of Canada. There were perhaps twenty priests present, as well as many lay brothers and gray nuns, who were all actively employed in their several locations. It was a sight well worth seeing, but I could not help painfully realizing the fact that I, a solitary clergyman of the Church of England, had to do my best, with little support and no personal help, amid a half-breed and Indian population, which was surrounded by Catholic influences. On that and every occasion when I have met the Roman Catholic Bishop and his people, I am bound to say that I have received most graceful and kindly attentions.

Near by the house which I occupied, and used for the services, was the Methodist chapel, with the parsonage attached. On my arrival the minister had been removed to Victoria, seventy miles down the Saskatchewan River, and another minister was expected, along with the chairman of the district. In due time these gentlemen appeared. The chairman was invited to call on the clergyman, but no visit was paid in response to the invitation, and in due time a report was sent to the Conference people in Ontario, to the effect that this gentleman had seen the sad sight, in the far North-West, of clergymen of the Church of England, both at Prince Albert and at Edmonton, 'working day and night, not so much to call sinners to repentance, as to make Ritualists of Presbyterians and Methodists.' By these people our work was looked upon as an interference with their rights, and our presence was simply shocking. We were regarded as poachers who plunder the preserves of respectable families in well-regulated communities. The spirit of Dissent seems to be the same all the world over. It cries out for liberty, and shouts persecution, whenever it has a chance in England ; and in the colonies, if it have in any respect the advantage of the Mother Church, it can put on the air of upstarts, and ape the manners which these, in popular estimation, are supposed to wear.

During this winter a most sad event occurred to Mr. McDougall, the chief Methodist missionary. He and his son were on the plains hunting buffaloes for their supply of meat. Towards the evening he left his son to seek the camp, that he might prepare supper. When his son arrived at the camp and called his father, he was not there. The night passed, and several days, and at last the body of the good missionary was found frozen, with the hands folded on the breast, and a calm smile upon the face, as if he had composed himself to rest. For his zeal in his work, and the manner of his death, the Methodists of Canada justly hold his memory in much respect and reverence.

CHAPTER V.

RIVER AND OTHER PERILS.

BY the summer of 1876 it had become evident that the neighbourhood of Fort Edmonton, on account of certain local circumstances and the paucity of the population, could not occupy the whole time of the missionary. He therefore enlarged his work, and visited all the Indian bands that he could find on the prairies. Some of the Indians told him that they had roamed for years without seeing the face of a missionary. If they came to Edmonton Fort to sell their furs, they might receive some religious attention, but such casual work could help them very little. These Indians had been morally influenced by a Mr. Wolesey, who had for years lived amongst them, and been as one of themselves. They had not at that time been gathered on reservations, but went where hunting was to be found. Often they asked me for teachers for their children, and for missionaries who would live among them; and their wishes were duly transmitted to the Church authorities, but with little immediate result.

Once, by special appeals to the venerable Society for the Propagation of the Gospel, I was able to get a missionary placed at Saddle Lake, more than a hundred miles from Edmonton, and thirty miles from any other mission-station, and at first the new mission seemed to be unusually promising; but the Methodist missionary, who had never held service there before, thought it becoming to visit the station regularly, and thus to sow contention, which resulted in the discouragement of our missionary and the final abandonment of the mission. Now, the Roman Catholics and the Methodists both have a station there, but the English Church has no representative in all that large district of country.

Also at this time I began my visits to Victoria, seventy miles away, by the invitation of the people there. These people had been brought up at our missions around the old Red River Settlement, Manitoba, and they had wandered eight hundred miles to find new homes. They were very poor, and not a thriving people, but some of them were very loyal to the Church of England, and wished the privilege of her services. I went frequently, until the cost of travelling and broken health rendered it impossible for me to undertake the long rough journeys. Many years have passed, and yet we have no missionary at Victoria.

On this journey I once nearly lost my life. Thirty miles from Edmonton is the Sturgeon River, on the old trail, and in the spring-time, after the melting of the snow, the river is deep and the current strong.

On one occasion, expecting difficulty in crossing this stream, I took two men with me, and on arriving there we found the river flooded. In one way and another the baggage was passed across, and also the horses and carts, and nothing was left but my light buckboard, in which I was to follow. I shouted for one of the men to return through the river, that he might drive me across, and by his weight in the vehicle help to balance it in the stream ; but he was positive there was no danger, and that I might expect to reach the other side safely. However, in coming to the centre of the river, the strong stream sent the buckboard rolling over and over again. The men were frightened, and rushed in to bring the mare and buckboard ashore, while I went floating down the stream. The men cried out, ' The mare is drowned !' but I exclaimed, ' Lug her to the shore, and quickly come to my assistance !' They did so, and with a long stick helped me to land. Not far off was the great Saskatchewan in full flood, against which I could have made no resistance.

On this road to Victoria, from Edmonton, were several streams almost as difficult to cross while in flood as this one, and, as I said, the journey there was expensive, and sometimes dangerous.

It may be interesting for clergymen ' at home,' who can travel by express trains, to know that on these journeys it is necessary to take most of our food with us, and many other things that we may require. A cart has to be loaded with a tent, bedding, saucepans, tin cups, plates, flour, tea, and whatever is required. In fine weather, if there are no mosquitoes, the journey is pleasant enough; but if it rains, and the unmade roads are knee-deep in mud, this kind of travelling will try a man's mettle. Nor does the trouble rest with the difficulties of the journey; after it the missionary is likely to find that the seeds of rheumatism and dyspepsia have been sown by the exposure and the badly-prepared food, so that his constitution needs to be unusually strong if he is to bear this kind of labour during many years. Yet it is, I suppose, by the same kind of experiences, and the same thankless toil, that the Christian civilization of our colonies is everywhere built up. Which will prove in the end to be the greater work—the heathen work or the colonial—we are not able to determine. They will both have vast issues in the Divine overruling; but when our colonies shall have blossomed into great nations, the work of the pioneer Church will fully justify itself, and receive its crown of honour and recognition.

CHAPTER VI.

SECURING A DWELLING-PLACE.

TO one coming from Ontario in these days it seems difficult to realize the fact that this North-West is not more modern than other parts of Canada. Excepting Quebec, the far North-West might be called the oldest part of Canada. Travellers reached these countries from Hudson Bay by the great rivers and lakes ; and very early in the eighteenth century the French Canadians, bent on discovery or trade, had visited the most distant places. For a hundred years Edmonton has been the centre of a large fur trade, where Crees and Blackfoot traded. Hundreds of miles were of no account to the natives, who travelled in large bands as convenience dictated. All places were the same to them if the hunt was prosperous, and they had ammunition and a few necessaries. Hence at the forts few Indians were seen, except at certain times, when they gathered from the plains, and pitched their tents and did their business, exchanging their furs for the things they required. Then they would disappear again for months.

As a rule, our food was very bad in those days; pemmican or buffalo meat, mixed with fat, was the great luxury. Our bread was made with soda instead of yeast; the commonest food was often unattainable. One day a man, four miles away, promised me a quart of milk if I would send for it. I was really yearning for milk, and was ill for the want of it. As soon as the boy was gone the eight miles for the milk, I placed myself at the window overlooking the road to watch his coming back, and as soon as he returned I divided it, and drank my share with the utmost greediness, as if my life depended on it. Such luxury was felicity.

A few months sufficed to reveal the real difficulties of my position as an isolated missionary. I had gone into a partly-finished log house, which I obtained by a mere accident; two hundred dollars of my own money had been spent in making the house at all habitable. We used the whole of the upper part for a chapel, and in fine weather it was very suitable, and looked very well; but in snowy weather the storms gave us great trouble. Often on Sunday mornings we had to use shovels to throw the snow out of the window; then, when the fire had melted the snow on the open rafters, the wet came down on our heads, and caused discomfort at the services. I could find no accommodation in the small log cottages close by. These generally consisted of two rooms, and were occupied by large families. In these there was little method of housekeeping, and no privacy. If I was to remain in

Edmonton, it seemed difficult to know what to do, for my house was held in a very precarious manner. One morning a neighbour, who was a trader, presented himself, and offered to sell me his house and land for a thousand dollars, as he badly wanted money. This seemed to be a Providential offer, for the house alone had cost that amount. On sending to the Church authorities, however, I could only learn that there were no funds available for such a purpose, and my affairs continued as unsettled as ever.

Since then the land alone has been sold for many thousands of dollars for building purposes, and funds have been secured for the building of a fine church, and the provision of an endowment for the minister in the town of Edmonton.

A little time after this a communication came to me from the owner of the house in which I lived, telling me that the use of the house was immediately required, and that he wished to have possession by ten o'clock the next morning. Of course I was a little surprised, as the house belonged to the chief trader, who was expecting to leave the Hudson Bay service. He had claimed three settlers' lots for himself and his brothers, but held them in a precarious manner; for the Canadian Government, in buying the Hudson Bay Company's interests in the North-West, had, in their bargain, included all Hudson Bay officers; and as these already had their share of the spoil, they were prevented from becoming settlers on their own separate account. These three lots led up to the Methodist mission property, and comprise a large part of the new town of Edmonton. It is a curious part of the local history which records that these lots were conveyed to other persons, and helped to make the fortunes, in one case, of two persons. If history, in small and large matters, were truly written, without gloss, and just as the facts occurred, what a commotion would be created, and how many would want it suppressed !

However, as I could not purchase a piece of land to build a cottage where Edmonton now is, I had looked about me for a 'location,' and I chose the Hermitage, where I now live, and I took possession of it a few days after receiving the notice above mentioned. It was in the middle of December, 1876, that I took up my permanent residence. A part of the summer had been occupied in clearing the spot of willows, and in building a small log house, for when I took shelter there—as Paddy says—there was no roof over my head, and no floor for my feet. It was with the greatest difficulty that I obtained lumber and shingles at heavy expense, and then I had to fetch them almost entirely by myself from a great distance, and to spend two nights in the snow in doing this team-work. Let those who suppose colonial pioneer missionary work is easy and luxurious, try it under such circumstances, and they will soon be converted to a more reasonable mind.

The Hermitage is situated on the North Saskatchewan river, about seven miles from Edmonton ;

it would in most countries be considered a pleasant locality. Around it are hills and valleys, trees and water. From it for twenty years missionary journeys have been made to settlements, and Indian tents, over a space of two hundred miles, and it has been the centre of all the work which one solitary missionary has been able to accomplish.

As this district is now well settled, it may interest readers to know one of my experiences on the first morning that I spent at the Hermitage in clearing the ground. We had pitched our tent in a valley by the brook, and early in the morning the boy came to the tent door shouting, 'Sir! sir! there is a man coming with cows.' The answer was, 'That is not possible, for where can he be coming from, and where can he be going to?' Around us there were no paths or roads of any kind, and the matter was dismissed from my mind. Soon, however, the voice exclaimed again, 'It is not a man; it is bears!' On looking from the tent, surely enough there were five bears—a large bruin, a black bear, and three cubs —quite near to us. Quickly I got a revolver and sharp knives, and, placing the boy behind me in the tent, I told him not to be frightened, but to do whatever he was told to do. The bears looked around unconcernedly for perhaps ten minutes, until the bruin led the way up a hillside, and they all disappeared. We never had visitors of any kind that we were more pleased to see quietly go about their business, as any accident might have brought fatal consequences.

Shortly after we took up our residence at the Hermitage, several events occurred indicative of the crude state of our civilization, and the lawlessness of the district. On my land I had a beautiful grove of spruce firs, and being fond of trees, I spent time and money in clearing the grove. Once, on returning home, I found persons had in my absence taken down the fence, cut down some of the trees, scattered the waste around, and carried the timber away. Presently I found the man who had done this wrong, and told him not to come on such business again. Instead of being ashamed, he told me he should do as he pleased with the grove, and 'that he should not hesitate to take it all away. When I complained to the only civil authorities we had, they replied that they had no instructions about Crown lands and timber limits, and so refused to give protection. Soon others came and did the same, and gave me to understand that they had the sanction of the local men, who did not recognise the right of anyone to a piece of land, or of what was on it. Out of this folly and injustice arose lots of trouble to the Canadian Government by 'claim-jumping,' which, as a piece of local history, may be mentioned in its place.

Just then there was a small band of American outlaws, and others, who stole horses and cattle, from whom I suffered, and could get no protection. Civil government could hardly have been more hopelessly inefficient in any part of her Majesty's Empire.

CHAPTER VII.

HALF-BREED RACES.

I T is now time to speak of the natives of the country among whom my lot was cast. These are locally known as half-breeds and Indians. Of the Indians some account will be given in a later chapter.

Our half-races are divided into English and French, chiefly because of their languages. Probably the French are the older people, for the French from Quebec found their way in early days up the Saskatchewan. These are Roman Catholics, and they chiefly live around the Catholic mission-stations. To see them turn out on some holiday occasion, one could fancy one's self in a French provincial town. Their manners are very French, and by no means ungraceful. Their French is that of the eighteenth century — country French with a mixture of the modern Parisian accent. All this is accounted for, partly by their French ancestors of Quebec, and partly by their education in connection with St. Albert's Mission. The women especially have

often very modest and pretty manners, and can
carry themselves with feminine dignity and pro-
priety. From early life they are cared for and
trained by the Grey Sisters, and, being naturally
imitative, they catch and retain nice modes of behaviour, which are quite a contrast to the surly
independent style sometimes observed in America,
the continent of liberty.

As a rule, the French half-races are not thought
to be thrifty. This arises partly from their circumstances. When they could freely go on to the plains,
and at any time get what meat they required, there
was little need for them to plan in order to secure the
necessaries of life. Now, however, they will have
the opportunity of developing the careful qualities of
their French ancestors, and we hope to see them a
prosperous people among the new communities of
this promising North-West. Undoubtedly they
need wise and disinterested guidance, and the control of an authoritative religion ; for the physical
life in the French half-race is very strong, and, like
all human qualities, can be rightly used or badly
abused. Their friends hope to see them take an
honourable place among the many and diverse races
who are now pouring into the pleasant Saskatchewan
country. The other half-breeds are called English
half-breeds, because they speak the English language,
or else are, in religion, separate from Roman
Catholicism. In fact, they are generally the descendants of Scotchmen or Orkney men who were in
the Hudson Bay service, and who consorted with

Cree women, sometimes giving them marriage and sometimes not. These matters will not bear close examination; but if facts could stand out clearly to human view, as they are in the sight of God, it might amuse some ethnologists, and shock others, to find the descendants of great names scattered abroad on these vast prairies, and sometimes called Indians, and sometimes half-breeds. I know half-breeds whom I respect very much, whose fathers went to Eastern Canada, or to England, and lived in respectable comfort with their newly-wedded wives, who never communicated with their children or recognised them in any way. Some time ago, on my way to Red Deer, I met a blind man led by his wife, and I was greatly struck with his fine appearance and dignified and graceful manners, of which, being blind, he seemed quite unconscious. On inquiry, I found him to be the son of a man bearing a well-known name in the North-West. He was begging for his living, and soon died in great destitution and misery.

My strong impression is that, for a hundred miles around these forts, the half-breeds are less Indian than they are generally supposed to be. Years ago the first mother would be Indian, then the next generation and the next would intermarry among themselves, and from these the Orkney men would take their wives, until the predominant quality would be Scotch. Somehow the Cree language has a charm for these people, and as the Cree is freely used with the English, the real ancestry of the people may be readily observed. Often when I visited Saddle Lake, more than a hundred miles away, an old man stayed with me who spoke only Cree ; if I had met him in an English village, I should not have questioned his nationality, even if he had used the English language as though it were his native tongue. One of the well-known Indian chiefs is undoubtedly of English blood ; another prominent man is the son of a Dane. Another of my friends interested me much. When I went into his tent, he was as polite as the patriarch Abraham could have been. He arranged the cushions carefully, and placed himself in an attitude of self-respect, yet of reverence, towards his visitor. With his observations he shrugged his shoulders, and spoke his Cree with a slight nasal intonation. His manner was that of a diplomatist, and I wondered where I had seen his face before, and the characteristic curl on his forehead, and then I thought of Disraeli (Lord Beaconsfield). This man's father was a French Jew, who was trading in these parts.

Hence it is not easy to classify the half-races in our North-West. An Indian now is a man who takes the treaty with the Government at Ottawa, and lives on a reservation. If he should neglect to do this he is a half-breed ; or if, having taken the treaty, he arranges to retire from it, he is ' half-race,' which in any case is probably his proper designation. Hence the relationship of these people to the Hudson Bay Company officials is a very close one. Many of them are their children; they have been their hunters or their freighters. It was the interest, and even the necessity, of both parties that they should stand well together. It would have been better if this relationship had been more remembered by the Hudson Bay Company when they transferred their real or supposed rights to the Canadian Government, by the permission of the English Parliament. No notice was taken of half-breed rights, French or English; they were all designated as Indian, a designation not true to the facts of the case, although convenient for Hudson Bay purposes.

Sometimes I see statements about the benevolent relationships existing between the Hudson Bay forts and the natives which surprise me; and I ask myself, What natives do they mean? Do they speak of their own kindred around the forts, or the hunters who are in many ways closely related to them? It would be strange if they were not humane to their own; but why should men of any class take credit for that? The fact is, the Hudson Bay Company was a trading corporation which existed for gain, and made it at any cost. They were no better and no worse than such corporations have always been, and are, in every part of the world. Their policy was not benevolence, but wealth; and the moral condition of the forts, and the character of the relationship between them and the natives of every kind, depended greatly on the individual men in charge of the forts, and their influence for good and evil. Visitors from a distance did not see everything—only the things that were not objectionable, and such as they might report at home. To read, for example, in the report of a lecture before the Colonial Institute in London, that intoxicating liquor was not even kept for private use in the interior Hudson Bay forts, for the sake of example to the natives, and that a challenge might be made to the world to show such high principle in a corporation, is simply preposterous nonsense. I have myself seen, in the Mountain Fort, a curious arrangement for serving out rum in trade with the Blackfeet, and near Edmonton Fort is ' Drunken Lake,' keeping up the tradition of Hudson Bay's most unholy rites—a tradition not likely to be soon extinguished.

Many of the most ancient Indian customs are still retained by the half-races, both French and English. Women prepare the food, and spread it before the men ; when all is ready they retire, and leave the feast for the lords of creation, and then afterwards eat what may be left. At first the visitor from a distance is not pleased with this custom, and seeks to change it ; but he finds it is of no use to interfere, and he soon quietly acquiesces.

The custom twenty years ago, even in the houses, was to spread the food on the floor, and to sit à la Turk—crossed-legged. Tables and chairs seemed unnecessary encumbrances.

Moss bags were in universal use for infants and small children, and the Egyptian mummy dress was exactly reproduced in the Far West. They also love horses, and dislike walking, except in hunting. Half-race people will walk miles to hunt their horses on the prairie, rather than go a small distance on foot to church. To ride to worship on Sundays seems to be a matter of dignity with them, and they attend to appearances. When they are in settlements that are isolated from the outer world, they practise the rites of religion. However, immigration soon changes their customs, and they quickly learn the ways of civilized white people. I know among them some of the most honourable men; and I have found some of them base and unprincipled beyond any power of description. If a half-race man is good, he is very good; if he is bad, he can be utterly depraved. In any case, he claims our pitiful interest, for if he be not enrolled as an Indian to live on a reservation, and so to receive the care of the Government and the benevolence of the Churches, he is left to fight his own way into a higher civilization, without settled habits to guide and support him, or the means of fulfilling the duties of the independent position after which he aspires. Hence he farms a little, and hunts a little, and freights a little, and manages something from day to day, and is so continually on the borders of starvation that, when an evil day comes, he falls into helpless suffering, to be caught by some disease which will soon take him off. Then, when a few years are passed, men ask where are the half-races gone? And how is it they disappear? Alas! it is as true here as everywhere—by cruelty and vice, or even by the well-meant benevolence of 'the higher race,' the natives of new lands are 'improved' off the face of the earth. It is a sad and mysterious story. All new creations seem to come into being through scenes of loss and pain, as the human race fulfils its destiny.

For twenty years I have laboured for the welfare of the half-races of the Canadian North-West, and it would have given me real joy to predict for them a splendid future. This is, however, quite impossible. In another twenty years their name may be only a memory.

Still, in the racial life of Canada, and all over the continent of America, their qualities will remain, and work to form the nations which will make the history of this 'New World.'

CHAPTER VIII.

INDIAN DIALECTS.

THOUGH original Indian types are not now abundant in the Canadian North-West, and students of ethnology should be careful as to the types of men chosen to represent the true 'red man' of America, enough of them remain to convey a distinct impression of their origin and history. Circumstances have given me fair opportunities of observing them.

In my old Muskoka mission I often visited the camps of Ojibwa Indians, and afterwards I saw a little of the Mohawks near Rice Lake, Ontario. Then, in my travels over the Great Lakes and by the Dawson Route, I fell in with Ojibwa, Iroquois, Swampy Crees, Plain Crees, Wood Crees, and Blackfoot. Natives also have come down to Edmonton from Athabasca, Peace River, and McKenzie districts, with whom I have lived in free communication; and on comparing their types, customs, dialects, as far as I was able, I cannot doubt the general identity of these people with one another, however mixed with the white race they may have become.

A careful scholar will find the logical form of the dialects the same, in their syntax, in the form of the verbs, and in their wonderful conjugations, which have an illimitable power of description, painting at once to the ear, noun, adjective, verb, adverb, time, place, and quality, even as the artist Turner threw his landscape on canvas to the eye, and as effectively describing the thing that is dealt with. Even now, after centuries have passed, there is a clearly per- ceptible connection between the sound of words. Should the student use his comparative philology in collating the dialects, he would see the dialects of England transfused; or he would notice how the German and English become allied in the transmis- sion of certain letters and their sounds; or he would recognise the laws of speech which divide, or unite, on a larger scale, the Indo-Germanic languages. Thus the *d* is often exchanged for the *t*, the *s* for the *sh*, etc.

The other letters, depending on mental laws which form sounds and arrange them into sentences, are transmitted and retransmitted, until from surface sound alone the dialects appear entirely different languages, though they are the same, or very nearly related, in the great groups of human speech. When the time comes for a great philologist—if it be not too late already—to collate the dialects of the American Continent, he is likely to see the identity of these, and to trace them to their source, viz., the uplands of Asia. Allowance must also be made for words retained or omitted—old forms and new forms —as in all dialects and languages.

Missionaries of repute do not always take this view of the Indian dialects. Archbishop Tache says:

' Each tribe talks a different language from any European ; different—with the exception of Esquimaux, perhaps—from Asiatic or African idiom ; different even from the language talked by other American tribes. Each of the races, even each of the tribes of Indians in the Northern department, uses a distinct dialect, as distinct the one from the other as French is from Chinese, or English from Hindustani.'

This is a specimen of the manner which is too often employed in these matters by persons of position, whose looseness of thought causes surprise, and even astonishment. The terms ' languages,' ' dialects,' ' idioms,' are all mixed up as if they meant the same thing.

Now, whatever may be the differences of French and Chinese, or of English and Hindustani, they are not dialects, but great languages, belonging to types of human speech that have little in common in their formation. French is a dialect formed by Indo-Germanic idioms, and Hindustani and English belong to the same great stem of languages, and they are all more or less allied. The Chinese language is not placed in this great class by any comparison at all. The Mongolian type of languages holds together by its similarity of arrangement, mode of formation, and methods of expressing sounds in speech after its own manner. It is my belief that learned research will prove that the Indian dialects are merely the dialects of Eastern Asia, transplanted to the American continent, and that the changes have been often less than is generally supposed, even in certain words which may be traceable to Mongolian roots.

Of these, almost daily I come across instances which cannot be accounted for by accident, such as the roots of words signifying common things—*e. g.*, water, river, fire, the names of objects connected with religion, and the names of places that are similar in Asia and America. Thus, the root *Ne*, or Cree for water (Nepe), forms the root of words in the bays of Japan. *Sepe*, or *Sebe*, is the root for the name of Siberia, or the land of rivers. The Calmucs and Cossacks gave the designation to that land of flowing streams, and the Calmucs and Cossacks and Red Indians have much in common in their language, physical aspects, customs, and religion. In the Cree and in the Mongolian dialects the letters *b*, *p*, and *d*, and *k*, *ch*, and *s*, *z*, are perpetually interchanged; hence the city of Sebastopol, Sepastibol, or Sevastopol, in the Crimea, connects the far East with the far West. Manchuria Maniteau. Also the sameness of the terms Manichou, Maintoo, Muanedoo, Manadeo, and Mandu, in Asia and America, signifying the same things, and connected with the same religious rites, cannot be overlooked. Likewise the names of

4

certain places on the two continents have a curious similarity, notwithstanding the blunders that are made in describing them on the maps that are now in use, viz.:

Jenissei, in Southern Siberia; Genisee, N.Y., U.S.A.

Geniseik, Siberia; Tennessee, U.S.

Moscow, Russia; Muskoka, Canada.

Sarces, Blackfoot Indians; Sarcis, South Russia.

Mississippi, river in U.S.A.; a bay in Japan.

Pe-chille Bay in China; Chili on the west coast of America.

Kichi Kulmagur, Indian and Mongolian for High or True Calmucs.

CHAPTER IX.

INDIAN RELIGION AND PARLIAMENT.

THERE are not existing now, among the North-West Indians, traditions respecting religion that are much worth attention. Paganism remains to some extent among tribes that are nominally Christian, but its rites are practised secretly. When hunters go on their solitary expeditions, they contrive to make some offering to the spirit which incarnates itself in the scenes about them, or in the objects of their pursuit; and they try to be on fair terms with the great evil spirit as a matter of policy; for the great good spirit is good anyhow, and won't harm anyone, while there is no accounting for Matchi-Manitou, who might be spiteful, and cause trouble and loss.

Here we have the remains of the old Shamaism of Asia, before Buddhism became mixed up with it or supplanted it. The ancient religion was clearly the ideal pantheism of the East, where all nature was poetized, and filled with a living, quickening, and ever-present spirit, representing the mental state of

4—2

the worshipper. Was he intelligent and pure-minded, then the conception and worship of the Great Spirit would be elevated, and orderly, and sustained by suitable rites. Was he passionate and of sensual life, he would cringe and bow to the evil spirit, and in worshipping become more debased through his superstition. The same things occur everywhere: in ancient India and Babylon, in Western Europe and America. Man, in forming his own religion, sees himself represented, and worships his own creations, which ever tend to become more and more like himself. It has been left to modern times and our advanced century to formulate this worship into a creed, a rite, and a religion, and to designate it, in pompous style, the worship or religion of humanity.

As yet no ruins of temples have been found in all this great region, nor is there any tradition of such buildings among any of the tribes that are now existing. The medicine-man of the conjuring type is all that is left of past times. This is what might have been expected from the circumstances of the people, if they came in isolated bands over Behring's Straits. Such expeditions were likely to be self-contained, whether they were voluntary or involuntary. The name Calmucs signifies a homeless people, wanderers, dwellers in tents, or roamers. Therefore they would not build towns or temples, even if the climate encouraged them. Agriculture is necessary before these things can be done. Towns depend upon agriculture, and temples follow established rites of religion and an organized priesthood. Hence we need not be surprised to find everywhere, on the northern parts of the continent, only burying-places, and places for defence and war. As tribes grew, and pressed on one another, conflict would be inevitable, and thus the wandering life would be perpetuated.

On our North-West plains there are still to be traced three types of the Mongolian race: the distinctly Tartar or Calmuc, comprising the Toou-Gooses, or Cossack type; next the Chinese type; and then the Japanese type. We have already mentioned the first, which on all sides forced itself on our attention. The second came almost as a surprise. In our second autumn here, the Indians met at Victoria, seventy miles north of Edmonton, and, to make the acquaintance of the whole band, I determined to be present when they received their treaty payments from the Canadian Government. Sitting in my buckboard to survey the scene more conveniently, and forgetting myself for the moment, I exclaimed to a friend: ' Did you see that Chinaman who has just passed ?' He lifted his finger, asking silence—for an Indian does not like to be observed; but, sure enough, there he was: the eyes, face, tawny skin, and braided hair hanging down his back, instead of pigtail—all proclaimed the Chinaman. Further observation confirmed the presence of this type among the Crees of the North-West.

The Japanese type is found more frequently in the mountains, and up the Peace River Country, though it is represented here. A family near me, who spoke Cree, out of charity took into their home an Indian child. She grew up, and I married her to a half-race man. She was a perfect Jap in height, with the characteristic dark tawny skin, oblique dark eyes, and Japanese nose and forehead. Her appearance was bright and intelligent, as if she had just come from Yokohama. Her brother was a Japanese student in University College, London. Corean faces as they are represented in pictures might well pass for Indian faces. There is little difference. The hammocks swung in a Siberian house, as cradles for children, are in no way different from those in Indian tents. Hudson Bay stockades and buildings are quite Siberian, and the Turkish bath may be seen any day in use on our prairies.

Undoubtedly there has been a great mingling of races in all parts of this great continent of America, although the type is mainly Mongolian from the North Pole to Patagonia. To one who has travelled, the difficulties of dispersion are not felt to be so very great. In all probability the Mongolian, under various designations, in ancient times wandered everywhere. From the uplands of Asia he filled China, and pressed into India, ancient Persia, Egypt, and Rome, both old and new. Probably the saying, ‘Scratch a Russian, and you find the Tartar,’ is true ethnological science.

The Mongolian could have got to America from the North-East or by Behring Sea. The Pacific Gulf stream could have borne him from Japan, or

from the coasts of China ; or, for that matter, mixed
with the Malay element in the course of centuries,
the isles of the Pacific might have been his highway.
The Mongolian race had the compass ; they were
expert in boat-building; they understood astronomy;
and as we become more fully acquainted with their
arts, it is seen that in many ways they were a wise
people. Great things were done in olden times by
simple means which we think to have been impossible under then existing conditions. If men could
build as they then did, and collect and polish precious
stones, and design ornaments, such as modern skill
cannot surpass or even equal, it is not unreasonable to expect that they were also acquainted with
the earth and the sea.

Suppose we had consulted the Arabs who travelled
up the Nile, and traded among the people of the
great lakes of Africa, would Europe have been so
long ignorant of those regions? And if China
claims to have sent her colonies to America in the
fifth, or even in preceding centuries, and to have
called the continent Fusang, why should we consider
the claim impossible or improbable ? The Chinese
profess to have a history of those events. Japan has
ancient maps on which a part of America is certainly
delineated ; and the Phœnicians, the ancient mariners,
have left their impress on every isle and continent
beneath the skies. When the temples and tombs of
Central America are carefully explored by scientific
men who are students of the arts, science, and
religion of the ancient nations, the unity of the race

of man is likely to become apparent, and disclosures will be made which will be of surpassing interest to those who are students of the earlier ages.

Tyre and Carthage and the Druids might well have planted Mexico, China, Chili, Sumatra, and Peru. The Siberians could have established Shamaism and Buddhism, by organized emigrations on the west coast of America. West of Selenginst is the seat of Kahma Lama, the rival of the Tibetan Lama, the old seat of mixed Shamaism and Buddhism—the typical religion of ancient America.

Emigrants from parts of Austria and the Crimea, and people from the Scotch Highlands who are familiar with the Gaelic, often remark on the similarity of the sound of Cree to their own languages; and it certainly has an affinity with Turkish and Hungarian; many of its root words are European, while the verb forms are a good deal like the Hebrew. Certain people look to America for the lost tribes of Israel; it is not impossible that some Jews may have found their way to it in the time of their world-wide dispersion, although there is no evidence of their presence. The religious rites and customs, especially of circumcision and blood feud, first-offerings and yearly festivals, were not peculiar to the Hebrews; they were customs very common in the East, especially in the first periods of human history, and were well known to, and practised by, the inhabitants of Mid-Asia. Likewise the tradition respecting a migration of Welshmen to America may have truth in it, especially if they took

their Druids with them, when the Romans were
hunting them out of existence in Great Britain.
They, with the Phœnician Baal-worshippers—who
were of the same priesthood—might have built the
temples and cities of Yucatan. The Welsh words
in Indian dialects may, however, take us far back in
the history of ancient languages.

Among Indian customs which are still retained,
although robbed of much of the ancient glory, is the
council Teppe, where the chief men assemble, and
confer on matters of importance to their people.
The Indian who is notified quietly attends his
parliament, and seats himself in silence. The chief
takes his position at the head of the assembly, which
is arranged in a circle, as if they were a band of
brothers. The speaker and medicine-man are on
his right hand. The pipe of peace is gravely filled
and lighted, and the chief passes it round, while all
is still in silence. This rite over, without hurry or
compromise of dignity, the speaker rises, and
narrates his description of the matter in hand, the
chief's and his own view of it ; for in this theocracy
king and priest agree before matters are formally de-
bated in council. Should the matter set forth be of
much interest, exclamations of agreement are heard ;
if the council be not all of one mind, it is silent
until another brave arises, and carefully unfolds his
view, approaching the subject with delicacy, and
presenting it in another aspect, without any asperity,
or rudeness, or gross personalities.

When all have spoken, or signified their assent by

'Aha! aha!' the assembly disperses as quietly as it came together; no formal vote is required, only the chief keeps a hieroglyphical record, if it may seem necessary. Changes are not hastily made, and only when the agreement is general is any action taken. If any differ from the general sentiment or opinion, there is no brawling; they quietly retire, and leave all action to those immediately concerned, or even drop off from the band and form relationships with another band of Indians. Indians have not as yet become civilized enough to enact the scenes which we sometimes read of in the big pow-wows of America and Europe.

Should any English Radical wish to study the elements of the Russian Mir, by way of introducing it into the social life of England, he may see it here in its different degrees of 'evolution.' The land is held in common by the tribe. At first they hunted on it in common; then, when they used any part of it for cultivation, the tribe owned the cultivated land; cultivation gave no individual right of possession; what was grown was usually shared among members of the tribe, as they often worked together or in bands. When cultivation increased, each person would take the piece of ground· allotted to him by the Indian council, and gradually the sense of right grew up, and every man who worked on land, and fenced it and improved it, was regarded as having a certain claim on it, which did not belong to others who preferred fishing, hunting, or conjuring; yet the tribe as a tribe were still masters of the whole, and the land could not be sold to, or used by, strangers without the solemn consent of the whole community. Were there a higher authority, as in Russia or the United States, the tribe as a whole would be responsible for its members, and the tribes would have in fact double laws and customs—those which existed in the tribe and bound the members together, and the laws that were enforced on them from without. These double laws and customs have, in America, been the cause of much misunderstanding and disputing, and often also the excuse for much cruelty and injustice, and the occasion of a bitter sense of wrong on the part of the Indian race. The East and West have met face to face, and the white man had no reverence or sympathy for what he saw ; conflict was inevitable, and the conquest of the red man was certain. Still, the idea of the sacredness of close human relationship which the Indian had, certainly as a sentiment, was true to human nature as a whole ; and the restlessness which is evident to-day among civilized people is caused by the absence of this sense, in their institutions, of the unity of tribes and nations, and the brotherhood of men in the same circumstances. ' Advanced ' statesmanship can now show its superior wisdom, by introducing laws and customs that will cover the whole life of a nation, as the Indian laws and customs united a tribe. But Europe cannot adopt the Russian Mir system ; the Indians themselves grow out of it as their social life advances. The Christian Mir is the true ideal for the happi-

ness and perfection of national life; it is brotherhood in Christ, and the rule that all men should be
members one of another.

In connection with this question—of the close
connection of Asia and America—it may not be
generally known that beyond the memory of man
the people of Siberia and North-West America have
traded together and been in free communication.
The island Imaklitt, one of the group of the Diomede,
was the centre of this trade, and thus Russia became the possessor of the great Alaska region,
which was afterwards transferred to the United
States.

CHAPTER X.

BUILDING THE FIRST CHURCH.

W E now resume the narrative of other events in our history. Our friend, the Chief Factor, was retiring from the Hudson Bay service, after many years of exile in these solitudes. He was not, as he told me, in sympathy with the prominent rulers of the company who were just then in power at Fort Garry, and he therefore sought retirement. Knowing the utter lawlessness of the country, and the general condition of affairs, he urged me to return with him, at least as far as Manitoba, until more settled times came and more favourable circumstances arose. This, however, could not be, and, bidding me farewell, he said with tears in his eyes:

'I do not like the idea of leaving you alone up here; it is not safe as things are.'

From the banks of the river I saw the boats which conveyed him and his luggage float down the stream with much regret, and I realized how lonely and utterly unprotected I was among strangers who were not in much sympathy with my work, or with the Church which I served. On arriving at Fort Garry, my friend found his wife in distress from the roughness of the persons who were then in power, and who had refused house accommodation to the Chief Factor's family until his arrival there. A beloved child had died, as he conceived, through causes connected with this harsh treatment. Surely this was not an ideal retirement after thirty-five years of solitary life, and often of separation from his family, to whom he was greatly attached. The Chief Factor was a man of noble presence, who wore the title ' Honourable,' as a gentleman should. His life was clouded by the dishonesty of a Canadian lawyer and M.P. This relative, and supposed friend, dissipated the earnings of his many solitary years.

During the years 1876 and 1877 a small church became absolutely necessary near the fort at Edmonton. We had held services in whatever houses could be obtained ; but sometimes the people were away on the plains freighting, or there would be sickness in the family, and the rooms could not be used for Sunday gatherings. But how were we to build, and where was the money to come from for building ? Ours was not an Indian mission, but a mission to settlers, and our people were very poor, and there was absolutely no money current in the country ; everything was done by barter, or in trade, as it was called. The only standard of value was skins—mostly beaver-skins—and it became a problem how to manage the finances of church-building

when there were no finances, and no skins to barter
for labour, or the means of labour. And where were
the materials for buildings to be obtained? or how
was even the ground to be secured on which a building could be safely erected? The question as to
who owned any land was a difficult one in those
days. The Hudson Bay Company were relinquishing
their rights—real and supposed—to the General
Government of Canada. That Government was
far off, and did not seem to know that it had any
responsibilities, or that people situated as we were
could possibly suffer any inconveniences. Surveys
were not made for several years, and no one knew
where his homestead was, or what land would be
allowed him when the surveys were made.

First we applied to a Hudson Bay officer, who
claimed lots, to give or to sell us a site for a church
and burial-ground, but we were refused; then we
sent our request to the gentleman who is now
Sir Donald Smith, who replied most courteously
that the company were then in treaty with the
Government of Canada for the transfer of all their
lands in the North-West, and that it was not in
his power to grant any land for public purposes.
However, a settler, a mile from Fort Edmonton,
very kindly allowed us from his claim five acres, for
which I gave him five dollars, as the only way of
defining the bargain, and securing the rights of both
parties (these five acres afterwards became nine,
when the surveys took place). I made an endeavour
also to secure a lot of a hundred and sixty acres for

Church property, but there were none at the time available for our purpose. The ground being secured, the next thing was to obtain building materials.

In the winter of 1876 the Bishop of the diocese for the first time visited the Edmonton district, and encouraged the idea of church - building. A committee of local men was consequently formed. The Bishop went away, but before he was out of sight, and even while the jingling of the dog-bells could be heard, the supposed chairman turned to me and exclaimed :

'Don't you suppose that I am going to act as chairman to a committee to build a church in such a country as this, and without means that can be depended upon. Who is to pay for it ?'

I pleaded with him that he ought to have told the Bishop that, and that his refusal to act now was not fair either to the Bishop or to me. However, the committee met once, and decided on the size of the building, and that it was to be of lumber. Months passed, and nothing more was done. Every now and then I saw reports in the newspapers of the influential committee which had been organized for church - building purposes at Fort Edmonton, and the reports sounded very grandly, so that I had to shield my eyes that I might not be mentally blinded by the glitter. As a matter of fact, the whole committee subscribed about thirty dollars towards the two thousand dollars which the little church cost. The business was abandoned as, under the circumstances, impracticable ; and there being no regular postal communications with my Bishop, I gave orders to have the frame erected for the sum of two hundred and fifty dollars; the man allowed ten dollars discount, and I myself paid two hundred and forty dollars, as a first personal subscription, hoping thereby to stir up the public generosity. Again the building was at a standstill, until the Church authorities sent the sum of five hundred dollars. Then, under the direction of the chief trader, men were provisioned and sent into the woods to cut lumber; and as flour was twenty-five dollars, or five pounds sterling, per hundredweight; sugar fifty cents, or two shillings, a pound; and nails fifty cents per pound, the five hundred dollars were soon spent. The shell of the church was nearly completed, the inner roof was bare, and there was no chancel end. The wages of the only man who would undertake the work ran up frightfully. Just then a Government saw-mill was being closed sixty miles above the fort. I bought a part of their lumber, enough to complete the building, and again this was my own personal subscription. By the earnest appeals of the Bishop of Saskatchewan, the Society for Promoting Christian Knowledge sent another sum of five hundred dollars, which the Bishop paid directly to the chief trader, and without any handling of mine. At the Bishop's request I afterwards handed to him, as the trustee of the diocese, the whole business. I was glad enough to be rid of the worry of debt, and of the hindrance which it had become to me in my work.

These matters require to be stated if the circumstances of a pioneer colonial missionary are to be
correctly narrated, or his work is to be understood
by persons at a distance. I have not pictured the
weary nights I spent in writing letters of appeal for
subscriptions to the leading people of the North-
West, with very little result; nor can I describe
the sacrifice of common comforts, and even of the
necessaries of life, which had to be made while these
burdens lasted. I had faith and hope enough to
bear them once; if I were called upon to pass
through the discipline a second time, I am afraid I
should lack the courage to make the attempt in
similar circumstances.

When any human work has to be done, in the
Church or out of it, the first thing necessary is to
comprehend the circumstances, and then to adapt
the means that are suitable in order to secure the
end that is in view. In most parts of the world,
that are in similar circumstances to Edmonton, a
mission would be first directed to the needs of the
natives, and then it would be purely a benevolent
enterprise. Such a mission is usually well supported; a house is erected for the missionary and
his assistants, and funds are sent for church-building; goods are supplied to him at the current rates,
and his way is cleared from embarrassments. Afterwards settlements grow up around the mission, and
after a varying number of years it will develop
into a self-sustaining mission. But if the Church
authorities begin missions to *settlers* before the time

for so doing is fairly ripe, and then try to throw upon them the difficulties of self-support, the attempt is sure to fail, and clergyman after clergyman will have to retire discouraged, perhaps with damaged reputations for zeal and energy, because they cannot do what is impossible under the circumstances, and what wisdom and good statesmanship would not have asked them to attempt.

At Edmonton, in 1875, the sparse population consisted of a few Hudson Bay employés, changing mounted police, roaming miners, and people who spoke the Cree language, and were half their time freighting on the plains. Real settlers only arrived years afterwards. Changes came, and then these matters fell into other hands. This church was subsequently sold by auction for fifty dollars, and used for a stable. It ought to have remained where it was built, and the ground around the church would have made an excellent Church of England cemetery.

CHAPTER XI.

THE FIRST BISHOP OF SASKATCHEWAN.

IN memory of those early years of my work at Edmonton, I wish to make a kindly record of several persons whom I then knew, who are now dead. The first is Colonel James Stewart, who was formerly well known in Manitoba. His decease took place at the Hermitage. He was originally a native of Quebec, and his father was a judge there. In early life he entered the Hudson Bay service, and travelled over the most northern districts. He also joined the search expedition under Dr. Rae to discover relics of Sir J. Franklin. He was a brave and kindly man, and the true friend of every one.

Also I remember, very tenderly, William Lenny, the blacksmith, a man of just mind and of a beautiful spirit, who was once my churchwarden. He made, and presented to the church, our first stove, with the necessary pipes, and placed them in position—a gift of love which I valued highly. He was born in the Orkney Isles, and I buried his body at Edmonton. But the most notable person I knew in my work was the Right Reverend John McLean,

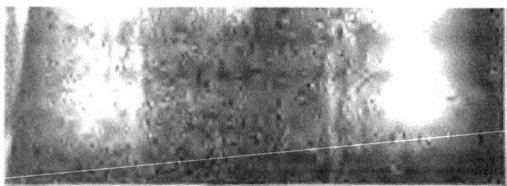

MCLEAN, FIRST BISHOP OF SASKATCHEWAN.

the first Bishop of Saskatchewan. Of this noble
and energetic Bishop, a well-informed correspondent
writes as follows :

' When the history of the Church of England in
Canada is written, it will have many a noble life to
record, many a deed of devotion, and many a life-
long self-sacrifice, worthy of Apostolic times. It is
impossible to over-estimate the permanent influence
of those who lay the foundation of Church work in
the various dependencies of the Colonial Empire, or
British Colonies. In the natural course of events
the men themselves pass away, but " their works
do follow them." The history of the Church in
Saskatchewan will ever be associated with the name
of Dr. John McLean, first Bishop of Saskatchewan,
who was born at Portsoy, Scotland, November 17,
1828. He graduated at the University of King's
College, Aberdeen ; was ordained deacon August 1,
1858; priest, December 15, 1858, by Dr. Cronyn,
first Bishop of Huron. He became Archdeacon of
Assiniboia, 1866 ; was consecrated Bishop of Saskatchewan, May 3, 1874; and died November 7, 1886.

' Several eventful years have now rolled by since
Bishop McLean passed to his well-earned rest—a
man of noble devotion, ceaseless energy, and un-
tiring perseverance. It may perhaps be difficult to
find a Bishop so fitted in every way to guide and
build up the work of a Church, amid the ever-
changing scenes and peculiar requirements of
Western life ; a man of boundless enthusiasm, full
of hope for the future, well expressing the genius of

the " Western pioneer's faith " in the land of "illimitable possibilities."'

'At an early period in the history of North-West
Canada, the foundation and corner-stone of mis-
sionary work was laid in the Red River Settlement.
On St. John the Baptist's Day, June 24, 1865, Dr.
Machray was consecrated as the second Bishop of
Rupert's Land, the consecrators being Archbishop
Longley, of Canterbury; Bishop Tait, of London;
Bishop Harold Browne, of Ely; Bishop Suther, of
Aberdeen; and Bishop Anderson, the first Bishop
of Rupert's Land. The diocese of Rupert's Land
then contained some two millions of square miles.
Beginning at the height near Port Arthur, it extended westward to the snow-capped summits of
the Rocky Mountains, southward to the boundary
line which divides the United States from Canada,
and northward without any defined limit. When
the Bishop of Rupert's Land reached the Red River
Settlement, after taking a survey of his work, he
determined to resuscitate the college begun by his
predecessor, and to establish a strong centre of
educational influence in connection with the church.
He offered the wardenship of his new college and
the archdeaconry of Assiniboia to his class-mate
and college companion, the Rev. John McLean, M.A.,
who was at that time connected with St. Paul's
Cathedral, London, Ontario, Canada West. The
Bishop of Rupert's Land, now Primate of Canada,
in his charge to the Synod in 1887, thus speaks of
his friend :

' " There is to myself personally, and I am sure to the members of former Synods, one great blank on this occasion. We miss the late able and energetic Bishop of Saskatchewan. The friend of my youth, whom I brought here to stand by my side, and with whom I shared the cares of the early years of my episcopate, he is naturally sorely missed by myself. For his own diocese his labours were abundant. The completed endowment of his see will ever remain an enduring monument of his worth. But such were his great and varied gifts, his readiness of utterance, and his unceasing devotion, that his death is a great loss to our province."

' The Rev. Mr. Wigram, the hon. secretary of the great Church Missionary Society, spoke thus of him in his sermon before the Synod:

' " When I left home last October, I looked forward with keen pleasure to being welcomed in Saskatchewan by Bishop McLean, that man of force and action who energized others by his own vigour, and knew difficulties simply as things to be overcome."

' A year or two passed quietly away in college work, and in the organization of the first parish in the embryo city of Winnipeg, Holy Trinity, of which the Archdeacon was Rector.

' It was in the last days of Hudson Bay rule, and political and stirring changes were at hand; the North-West territories were transferred to Canada, but Canadian rule was not established without bloodshed and difficulty. Archdeacon McLean was faithful at his post during these days of trouble and political unrest; we find him beside the prisoner, and those who were condemned to death.

'Gunn's History states :

'"As soon as Major Boulton was safe within the walls of Fort Garry, he was placed in irons, a court-martial was held, he was found guilty of treason against the Provisional Government, and sentenced to be shot at noon the next day; but at the intercession of the Lord Bishop of Rupert's Land, Archdeacon McLean, and, in short, of every influential man among the English, and I have been told also at the earnest entreaty of the Catholic clergy, the execution was delayed till midnight of Saturday, the 19th. Riel, apparently, kept his determination to have Major Boulton shot up to ten o'clock on Saturday night, two hours before the execution was to have taken place, and Archdeacon McLean had spent nearly twenty-four hours with Major Boulton, administered the Sacrament to him, and prepared him to meet his fate. At length Riel yielded to the entreaties of Mr. Smith (now Sir Donald Smith), and agreed to spare Boulton's life. He immediately proceeded to the prison, and intimated to Archdeacon McLean that he, Riel, had been induced to spare Major Boulton's life, and had further promised that, immediately on the meeting of the Council, which was shortly to be elected, the whole of the prisoners would be released, requesting the Archdeacon at the same time to explain these circumstances to Major Boulton and the other prisoners."

' Major Boulton is now a distinguished member of the Senate of Canada.

'Archdeacon McLean was requested, by the Dominion Government, to take a tour through the older provinces, and lecture on the North-West. His glowing description of the Western prairies, his enthusiastic faith in the future of North-West Canada, was of great service in exciting an interest in Manitoba and the North-West, and in directing the attention of the Canadian public to the boundless capabilities of this Western El Dorado.

' During this tour he collected a large sum of money for St. John's College, Winnipeg. Manitoba and the Territories now entered Confederation. The prospects of settlement and development of the North - West necessitated the reorganization of Church work. The huge diocese of Rupert's Land was divided. Bishop Horden was appointed to Moosonee, Bishop Bompas to the Mackenzie River, and Dr. McLean was consecrated by Royal mandate at Lambeth, May 3, 1874, to the bishopric of Saskatchewan.

'One might well have hesitated before undertaking a work of such difficulty. In more modern times, when a Bishop is appointed, he usually reaps the benefit of the labour of his predecessor : he finds endowment for his support secured, Church work organized, and Church institutions established. But such was not the case with Bishop McLean. Everything had to be begun *de novo*. There was no episcopal endowment. There were just two

missionaries in his vast jurisdiction, extending from
the Rocky Mountains to Lake Winnipeg.   The year
after his consecration one of the two missionaries
died.   There were other difficulties to contend with.
There were no railroads in those days.   The Bishop
had to undertake the journey of five hundred miles
with dog-cariole in mid-winter in order to reach his
diocese, camping each night in the snow, with no
friendly shelter save the canopy of heaven.   The
thought of one day reaching Saskatchewan in a
" Pulman " was not even within the reach of the
wildest flight of imagination.   The very idea of a
sleeper, and the ubiquitous porter, would have
been considered the inauguration of an episcopal
millennium.   In his first journey the Bishop travelled
two thousand miles with the thermometer often
registering 40° below zero.

' In 1878 the Bishop visited England with the
intention of raising further funds for the bishopric
endowment and for other objects.   It may here be
stated that the Society for the Propagation of the
Gospel most kindly and generously allowed the
Bishop two hundred pounds per annum, to enable
him to carry on his work, and they continued this
as long as the Bishop required it.   Although many
tried to dissuade the Bishop from attempting to
collect funds, owing to the very great depression
prevalent at that time, he was not daunted, and the
enthusiasm of his words, and the single-heartedness
of his devotion, soon made him many friends and
supporters, and he returned to his diocese with a

considerable part of the necessary episcopal endowment funds, for missionary and educational work,
and for building. He made his headquarters at
Prince Albert. Emmanuel College was built, and
opened in 1879, as the first institution for higher
education in the diocese. Several of the missionaries
of the North-West were trained there. The Bishop
took part in the college work as the Professor of
Divinity. The Bishop had an Act passed, by the
Dominion Parliament, for establishing a University
of Saskatchewan, and no doubt he would have
secured funds for endowing it had he lived. His
great desire was to have an educated clergy. In his
last address to the Synod, on August 4, 1886, he said:

' " I earnestly hope that the clergy will try to follow
the advice now given. I think it right to state that
I am so strongly impressed with the importance of
encouraging steady and systematic study in those
branches that tend to equip a clergyman for
thoroughly discharging the duties of his office, and
so convinced that those who are content with just
study enough to pass the examination for Holy
Orders cannot really fulfil their functions thoroughly,
that, while God spares me as Bishop, I shall make
this consideration a very influential one in determining questions of promotion, as far as these
questions lie within my influence."

' In the same address the Bishop thus spoke of
Emmanuel College :

' " The college is also becoming the mainstay of
the diocese for the supply of clergy for the settle-

EMMANUEL COLLEGE, PRINCE ALBERT, NORTH-WEST TERRITORIES.

ments. Already four out of the six most important towns in the diocese have, as their clergymen, men who received their training at the institution, and these are working to my entire satisfaction, while several less-prominent posts are most worthily filled by its former students."

' It perhaps should be stated that the Bishop was approached on the subject of accepting one of the older dioceses of Eastern Canada ; but he was faithful to his Western diocese.

'The Bishop was in the town of Prince Albert during the rebellion of 1885. No one who was in Prince Albert during those days of danger and anxiety will ever forget the Bishop's sermon on the Sunday after the Duck Lake fight. The North-West Mounted Police and the local militia were drawn up in the square. The Bishop took his stand under the flagstaff in the centre, and, in words of patriotic eloquence, spoke of the noble citizens of Prince Albert who had fallen in the Duck Lake field of battle, of the glorious traditions of British law and justice, and of his faith in the permanent stability of the Canadian Dominion.

' In the autumn after the rebellion the Synod met. It was the Bishop's last Synod, and in his address he said :

' " Since we last met I have been able to visit, and hold Confirmation, in every mission in the diocese but one, and this will be shortly visited. In the great majority of cases I have made at least two visits to each mission."

' After the Synod was over, although he was not in good health, he started on a long visitation of the diocese.   In his diary he writes as follows :

' " *Monday, August* 16.—Left home with Hume."

' " *Tuesday*, 24th.—Reached Calgary."

'On the 29th he received a telegram telling of the birth of his son, but sent word that he must push on for Edmonton, as his work must not be neglected, and he would return as soon as possible.

' " *Sunday, September* 5.—Confirmation in All Saints' Church, Edmonton.

' " *Monday, September* 6.—I did not feel well to-day, but started on our return journey.   On going down the hill near the fort we met a cart, and, there being no room to pass, our waggon was upset, and we were all thrown out.   We, however, proceeded on our journey soon after ; but I became seriously ill, and after proceeding five miles we returned to Edmonton, where I lay for three weeks at the Ross Hotel under medical charge.   I became very ill and very weak; I sent back our team to Calgary on the second day.   By the doctor's advice I had a large skiff built by the Hudson Bay Company, with the stern part covered with canvas like a tent.   Two men were engaged to conduct it to Prince Albert, a distance of six hundred miles by water.   We reached Fort Pitt on Thursday, October 7, exactly eight days from Edmonton, which we left on September 29. Hume gave great help in working the skiff, and was most kind and attentive to me, both at the hotel and in the skiff.   I continued very weak until we reached

Fort Pitt. During the last two days I have been feeling much better, and am now writing up this note-book in the wood on the river bank, where we have taken refuge from a cold head-wind. Our progress is slow; we may have snow and ice in a day or two. I think of going overland from Battleford."

'The Bishop was so ill when he reached Battleford that he was obliged to remain in the skiff, and his son Hume feared that he would not live until he reached Prince Albert. The weather was bitterly cold, ice having begun to form on the river; however, the men worked very hard, assisted by Hume, a lad of fifteen, who did all he could for his beloved father, whom he described as so sweet and patient in all his pain and weakness. He was constantly singing to himself during the weary hours of night. This dear son, Hume Blake, died at Athabasca Landing, May 16, 1893, in his twenty-second year.

'After the Bishop's return home he rallied considerably for a few days, but he was too much weakened by the hardships of the journey. Fever set in; he was delirious at times, but even in his wanderings his beloved diocese occupied his thoughts, and at times he imagined himself conducting meetings with his clergy.

'On Saturday afternoon, November 6, he spoke in the most eloquent manner of the future of the diocese; then he kissed all his loved ones, and shook hands with others who were with him. As the sun was setting, he asked his daughter, Mrs. Flett, to help him to sit up, and had the blinds

drawn up so that he could see the sunset; then he
said :

' " Do bring lights ; it is growing very dark."

' From that time he spoke but little, but appeared
to be in a sort of stupor, from which he was roused
to take stimulants. About 5 a.m. on Sunday morning his wife was standing beside him, and he said
to her : " My lips are getting so stiff;" and then he
kissed her, with loving words of all they had been to
each other. He did not speak coherently after that,
but became unconscious, and remained so, surrounded by all his family, until 12 a.m., when he
fell asleep like a little child.

' He is buried outside the chancel window in
St. Mary's Cemetery. His monument bears the
following inscription :

' " Entered into the rest of Paradise, November 7,
1886, John McLean, first Bishop of Saskatchewan,
in his 58th year.

' " I believe in the Communion of Saints."

' Bishop McLean did much for Prince Albert. In
addition to the fine buildings on the college property,
he raised money to maintain and carry on the work.
Then he lived in Prince Albert, and helped it in
every way that he could. Bishop McLean only
enjoyed the full interest of the Bishopric Endowment Fund for a short time before his death. The
Bishop devoted an hour each day, when at home, to
reading the Service for Consecration of a Bishop,
and in seeking strength and help to live up to, and
in every way to be faithful to, the vows which

he had taken. He often said he felt appalled when he thought of the immense responsibility of his office.

'So lived, and so passed away, this great and good man, who has been sorely missed by the Saskatchewan and Calgary dioceses, especially in their efforts to overcome the financial difficulties that are incident to all new Church work in countries where there are no endowments for religion, and the people are too poor to do much for Church support. Such dioceses require exceptional men, and Bishop McLean was an exceptional man. For his diocese of Saskatchewan the Bishop raised, clear of all expenses, the following funds:

	Dollars.
'Bishopric Endowment Fund	73,140.26
Divinity Chair, Emmanuel College ...	10,023.42
Louise Scholarship	340.00
W. McKay Scholarship	700.00
Clergy Endowment Fund :	
(a) General	4,000.00
(b) Stanley Mission	260.00
(c) Devon Mission	884.22 '

CHAPTER XII.

RIEL'S REBELLION.

IN the years preceding the rebellion of 1885, there was much unrest in the Edmonton district; dissatisfaction with the Dominion Government was nearly universal; their agents were generally unpopular; settlers could get no attention to their complaints, and no one felt safe in any of his land transactions. A case arose in which a settler tried to defend some of his property from depredation, and he was fined by the stipendiary magistrate for attempting his own protection. There seemed no recognised law, except the decision of a magistrate, and no one could tell what this would be, or the code that might rule him. There was, in fact, no law, although there was supposed to be a Government.

We were not in Ontario, or Quebec, or Manitoba; we were in an undefined territory, subject to the man who happened to be in office, and he was a great distance from his superiors, and found no difficulty in shielding himself behind his own reports. If a man took a pair of stockings from the Hudson

Bay store, he was quickly arrested and punished; but if he trespassed on land, and cut down timber of great worth to the settler who had fenced it and protected it from prairie fires, the settler was informed that he had no property in the soil or in the trees, and that he had no protection for the labour or expense that were invested in his claim or real estate. Blackstone teaches that men have natural rights to the lands which they use, so long as their rights do not infringe on the claims of others; and surely under the British flag these natural rights should be allowed. Yet in the Edmonton district these were denied, with the result that the lawless attempted to 'jump' the lands that were possessed by others—that is, to publicly steal them. Exhibitions were thus made of the greed of lawless human nature that were sad indeed to behold.

Outside the circle of Government men, a Committee of Public Safety was instituted, and it seemed necessary, if the commonest order was to be observed. Persons had become possessed of pieces of land where the town of Edmonton now stands; some had paid money for them, and others had put buildings on them, and claimed the right to do so. But it might be asked, Where were the Government during all this time? The answer is: At Ottawa, drawing their salaries, amongst other things, for governing the North-West. For a long time there were no authorized surveys, and confusion was rampant.

One day a court was held in order to try certain men, some of them being our most respected citizens.

A would-be thief of landed property had put a building on another man's lot, hoping thus to get possession of it for himself. The proper owner removed
the building, and placed it so near the high banks of
the Saskatchewan that it, by design or accident,
rolled over, and the man was put to great trouble in
recovering even a part of it. The lawless man sued
the removers, and got judgment so far that the
owner was fined for causing unnecessary damage in
the removal of the house; the inference being that,
if he had removed it and no damage to it had
followed, the action would have been lawful. No
distinct instructions, however, were given from the
bench, and matters continued as unsettled as before.
The lawless saw that there was very little to restrain
them, and they acted accordingly.

But why was this allowed? Possibly in order that
the Government men might have a free hand to do
what they liked in the issue of patents, claiming the
lands of the great North-West as purchased property,
through their transactions with the Hudson Bay
Company. According to their view, no one had any
rights. All conditions of men were in the same
position; half-breeds, and settlers, and even Indians
who did not take the treaty, had no legal standing,
save as British subjects. England was a long way
off, and Canada lay between the two, and effectually
hindered the cry for justice reaching the motherland.

If an able Commissioner from England had been
sent to the Indians, half-races, and settlers of the

North-West during the three years preceding the events of 1885, there would, in all probability, have been no outbreak. Millions of dollars and many valuable lives might have been saved. Order would have been preserved, based on respect for Governmental authority and its necessary institutions. The authority of the Ottawa Government is not strong enough in these territories, and it has not on all occasions the will to enforce obedience to its own orders. When, in 1891, it attempted to remove its land office across the Saskatchewan to the railway terminus, an armed crowd of men and boys successfully resisted the order, and that in the open daylight.

While these uncertainties were occurring, about the land claims of natives and settlers in the Edmonton district, land speculators were busy, and very successful, in their greed for spoils. A company was set going with a grand name, ostensibly patronized by the Ottawa Government supporters. It proposed to colonize, and bring both settlers and capital into the country. Large tracts of fine land were entrusted to the company, but they brought no settlers, and to-day their buildings are in ruins, and most of their lands are waste.

Meanwhile, honest settlers were compelled to go far into the wilderness for homesteads, and business and civilization were hindered in order that these speculators might make money by the labour and enterprise of neighbours who were cursed by their presence. A poor man is sharply looked after if he

do not fulfil his engagements on his land claim, and
his titles are cancelled. How is it, then, that
fraudulent companies can hold their own, or, rather,
the lands that should belong to other people?
Governments in these days are, in theory, governments for the people by the people. As population
increases here, some of these questions may receive
stern answers.

While these things were occurring among settlers
in every part of the North-West, the Indians also
were becoming very restive. Most of them had
their reservations, and the agents, as a rule, had
dealt fairly by them. Often, however, these agents
could not keep their word to the Indians, because of
the distances over which supplies had to travel, or
because of misunderstandings at Ottawa. Some of
the Indians also misunderstood their treaties, or, at
least, thought that they had been over-reached in
their bargains. Possibly their intercourse with a
low class of traders did not tend to increase their
contentment, and from causes of this kind the
rebellion of 1885 arose.

Unrest seemed to be in the air, as when a storm
is brewing, and the clouds are preparing for a furious
tempest, yet no one knew where the centre of the
storm would be, or when it would burst. Mysterious
rumours came to Edmonton of what would happen
when the grass was green—that is, when Indian
horses could travel and find pasture on the plains.
Then came the news of the massacre of the Roman
Catholic priests and Indian agents at Frog Lake.

Then of the fight at Duck Lake, where the mounted police and volunteers scarcely held their own.

Then Canada was aroused, and sent Middleton and troops, and the news came of the battles of Cut-knife Creek and Batoche on the South Saskatchewan. By this time the Indians were in a ferment everywhere, and at Battleford they were committing depredations which could not be resisted. Inspector Dickens also had abandoned Fort Pitt, and plunder was the order of the day. All over the plains the strangest rumours flew with the speed of lightning; they came to Edmonton from east, west, north, and south, and we could not tell what was about to happen. In all directions were Indians enough, if they were well led, to try the mettle of our sparse and scattered settlements, and our people were virtually without arms and ammunition. They were almost entirely unprepared to fight for their own lives, or for the honour of the Government. Centres were formed at St. Albert's Roman Catholic Mission, Fort Edmonton, and Fort Saskatchewan, and most of the settlers left their homes and took refuge in these places. They were prepared for defence as efficiently as circumstances allowed. Often, judging from rumours that arrived, our lives and homes were in peril. Repeatedly it was rumoured that bands of Indians, several hundreds strong, were close at hand, and were fording the river a few miles up the stream, on their way to attack Fort Edmonton.

The sudden rise and growth of rumours on these

plains is beyond belief, and every new story is somehow or other believed, simply because there is no
evidence to the contrary. Thus, one Sunday, at All
Saints' Church, the story went round that the
Indians were crossing the river at the miners' flat,
seven miles off. When the service was ended, and
the people had gone to the fort for refuge, I went to
my residence, seven miles off, to see if I could hide
some of my most valuable books before the Indians
could scatter themselves, and proceed to burn up
and destroy everything they came across. Two or
three miles out I met a scout from the prairies, who
confirmed the rumour, and said that the Indians
were now probably near the fort and preparing to
attack it. For a moment I thought of my books, but
then I thought of the women and little children to
whom I ministered, so I immediately returned, to
find that the excitement was still very great, and
that all things were in readiness for a flight to some
solitude in which the women and children might be
preserved. Happily, however, on this occasion the
Indians did not appear.

The truth is, that the rumour had some foundation, for the Indians around had left their usual en-
campments, and had hidden themselves in places
where they could be found by messengers from a
distance, and they were undoubtedly only waiting
for a general rising, and many of them were certainly
ready enough to do any mischief that came in their
way. If Riel had been victorious at Carlton, very
few white men would have been left alive in the

distant settlements. The entire Indian population would have been aflame with the passions of greed, and lust, and murder.

How far the half-races, especially the French half-breeds in the Edmonton district, were originally mixed up with the early stages of the rebellion, is a difficult and intricate question. Riel certainly had the sympathy of many of them. Dumont himself was from our neighbourhood, and had friends here. The mistake which Riel made in his tactics was the mistake of a man of very limited information and of great self-esteem. He did not know the outside world against which he arrayed himself; he did not realize that behind Canada was England. He posed as a liberator, as a kind of Garibaldi, or Arabian Mahdi. He wanted to be a prophet, the founder of a new religion—a Moses on a small scale, who would lead his people into their own possession, and drive out the nineteenth-century Canaanites. He did not disclaim the murder of the priests at Frog Lake, and he separated the men under his influence, as much as he could, from the Roman Catholic Church. By such a policy he could not possibly succeed; and he destroyed the sympathy of a powerful organization which might have been interested in any grievances which the Metis had, and have given them a certain protection. Moreover, his folly alienated his cause from the French province of Quebec, which could have afforded him powerful support, and given great trouble to the whole Dominion of Canada. As it was, the brave

and skilful defence which Dumont made with his
badly-armed band of five hundred undisciplined men
produced a great impression; and it might easily
have grown into a war of races, which would have
challenged the sympathy and chivalrous feeling of
ancient France. A little spark sets the prairies
ablaze, and a few men speaking French, and conducting themselves bravely, and struggling with a
real grievance against great odds, might have touched
the honour of France and brought her back to
America again. Riel's ineptness crushed the Metis
and annihilated all external sympathy.

Thus, in the Edmonton district, while we had
rumours and anxiety, we had no actual difficulties.
Some Metis were sullen, and the Indians whom we
met scowled, but no shot was fired in anger. Probably the Indians' friends did not think themselves
strong enough to cope with the mounted police.
A home guard had been enrolled, but outside assistance did not arrive until later. The citizens of
Edmonton cleared the brush and trees from their
streets, because an enemy could hide and fight in
ambush behind them, and, calling a meeting, they
sent a special messenger one hundred and ninety
miles to Calgary, where the Lieutenant-Governor
happened to be, urging immediate assistance before
it was too late. The messenger, who was a native
of the country, rode through the Indian reservations,
exposing himself to much danger, and attracting
attention by the speed at which he travelled. Sometimes he was followed, but, being well mounted, he

distanced his pursuers, and, scarcely resting or changing horses, in less than two days he covered the one hundred and ninety miles, and told the story of the stern needs of Edmonton. Already Mr. Dewdney, the Lieutenant-Governor, had arranged with General Strange—a most capable officer who had seen service in India—to proceed north to Edmonton. The news of his coming kept the disaffected quiet, and probably saved the district from an Indian war. His column was made up as follows :

Strange's Rangers, 50 ; police, 67 ; 65th Battalion, 332 ; Winnipeg, 332 ; P. Battalion (92), 307.

Afterwards the 65th regiment of Montreal, under Colonel Oimet, was stationed at Edmonton, while General Strange went east after Big Bear, who made for Battleford, where General Middleton was, and gave himself up. Thus Indian and half-breed hopes of driving away the white man from the North-West Territories, and possessing the country for themselves, were crushed and destroyed for ever. Riel was hanged at Regina, N.W., on September 18, 1885.

CHAPTER XIII.

THE CAUSES OF THE REBELLION

THOSE who would understand this so-called 'rebellion' must have a distinct idea of the circumstances that led up to it. It is not sufficient to say that it was 'pure cussedness' on the part of the half-breed and Indian. In former pages I have endeavoured to convey the impression that the confusion was not all their fault, by pointing out the genesis of the outbreak. History will, I believe, assign the following causes: First, and chiefly, the utter inattention of the Hudson Bay officials to the interests of the half-races, when they negotiated for the transfer of the territories to the Government of Canada. In different parts of the North-West, settlements had arisen around their forts, and many half-breeds were scattered in all directions on the plains, who were living an independent life as hunters, trading with the forts, and exchanging their buffalo meat and skins for the things they required. How did this half-race spring into existence? Surely from the presence of Hudson Bay or North-West traders. They were, in fact, the children and wards of that great company, and they comprised a very large part of the population of these territories in later years. If this be correct, and I believe it is, how could the Honourable Hudson Bay Company fairly overlook the interests of this considerable population, and make no provision in the transfer for their legitimate claims? Was it intended to keep their claims in abeyance? Or did it arise from pure contempt of the half-races, who were their own descendants? The half-race could not understand its position; it was in itself helpless; it might send its complaints and its petitions, but they would only be treated with indifference and contempt. The Hudson Bay Company had influence and wealth to support its case both in England and in Ottawa; but what could the half-race do, who were so far off, and neither had advocates to plead their case, nor money to pay them for their labour and ability, if they could have been found? The historian who wishes to trace events to their true causes must hold the official negotiators of this transfer greatly responsible for the unrest, the uncertainty, and the waste of money and lives, which are associated with the scenes of 1885.

Secondly, there was often a great want of tact and prudence on the part of the Canadian gentlemen who had, in different ways, to do business in these parts, and more especially with the tribes on the plains. Before any arrangements were made with the Indian bands, surveyors were sent to survey longitudes, etc., and these surveyors puzzled the Indian. When he inquired the reason of their visit, and asked whether the great Queen-mother had sent them to do their magic in the country, he was informed that the Canadian was master now. But since the transfer has puzzled wise heads on both sides of the Atlantic, there is little reason for wondering that the Indian could not see through the fog. Company power gone, Queen-mother made light of, Canadian rule set up from beyond the Great Lakes. What was about to happen now? Add this to the half-race grievance, and it is not surprising that in time the fire should blaze on the prairies until much was consumed. There was altogether too much contempt for the Indian and the half-breed, and too little attention given to their customs and manners. The Indian is very formal, and precise, and dignified, in his ways and ideas; he is easily pleased, but soon offended; and what may seem to be trifles will give great offence, which will not soon be forgotten.

On several occasions I ventured to mention these matters privately to gentlemen who I thought were overlooking them in their transactions, and un-necessarily producing discontent. But the answer always was, ' What do I care? I am not afraid of an Indian!' Some of these gentlemen were pretty well scared afterwards. But others had to meet the expense, and to sacrifice their lives, and to bear the penalty of their incompetence. On one occasion I was present at an Indian treaty payment before the outbreak. The rumour was that the Indians were much dissatisfied with the way their treaty arrangements were kept, and that they intended to express this dissatisfaction before they took their money. The scene itself was interesting to anyone who sympathized with human life in any form. The Government men, visitors, and traders took their station on an elevated position; far down in the valley the Indians had arrayed themselves in all the glory of their paint and feathers. On their approach they danced their dances and fired their guns, by way of salute and respect to the great man. Then the colloquy began. 'Are you the great chief who is able to attend to our wants and complaints?' The answer was, 'I am.' Then various matters were discussed, and complaints were made. That day the Indians would not receive their money. Perhaps half an hour was taken up with a discussion as to whether twenty pounds of tea should be allowed them while in the summer they were cutting their winter's hay, and this tea was not very graciously refused. Suppose this gentleman had known their temperaments, and had even, as a personal gift, shown his interest in them by giving them this small quantity of tea, their delight would then have been unbounded. Afterwards, through the private persuasion of wiser and more kindly disposed persons who were not in office, the Indians did, with reluctance, take their treaty money.

Thirdly, difficulties of all kinds on account of distances were sure to arise, and these could scarcely be avoided in the transmission of ploughs and other instruments of industry. The Indian had been promised these things, and oftentimes they did not arrive. Patience was needed on both sides, but especially wisdom on the part of the 'white man,' if matters were to run smoothly. Manner here, as in other lands, was often of supreme importance to a good understanding. Contempt of persons and races is never good policy, and it is to be hoped that when the Athabasca, Peace River, and Mackenzie River districts are opened up for settlement, these lessons will be remembered, and all collisions of races avoided in the future.

CHAPTER XIV.

TRUE AND FALSE BRAVERY.

IT is in scenes such as we have described that human nature shows itself, and the qualities of men are exhibited. Some in our small communities at this time said but little, and were quiet in their manner, but were men of real mettle. Others primed themselves with whisky in order to keep their courage up. When the danger was over, it was surprising to discover how many brave men we had amongst us, and what heroic deeds would have been done if only opportunity had offered. Perhaps it is as well that the heroism was not put to the test by grim Indian warfare. The courage thus saved may be retained for other occasions in life's battle, where it can be used daily in all sorts of ways, and to our life's end. Courage physical, courage mental, courage moral—of each and all of these we cannot have too much, in order to make the truly noble character.

One Saturday, during the height of the excitement, a secret message came to me from an Indian girl, to whom I had ministered in her illness, when her tent was pitched near the fort. Her people had taken her with them to their hiding-place on the plains, but she felt that she was dying, and longed to see a clergyman. In her forlorn condition she begged me to visit her, and prepare her for the end. It was miles away, and I could not find the place alone, for it was in the wild wilderness, which was without roads, or, indeed, any marks that would guide me. I spoke to several persons who professed to know the place, and who said that they could conduct me. I made an appointment with one of the bravest to start with me immediately after the Sunday morning service. The service over, and the horse harnessed, I waited for my guide; but I waited in vain: he did not appear, nor could he be found anywhere. I sent after one and another person, who the day before had said that they knew the place well, and were not afraid to go; but it was always with the same result. These brave men thought a stray bullet from an Indian gun might find them, and they regarded discretion as the better part of valour. The poor girl died in her loneliness, and they made her a solitary grave somewhere on the wide prairies, where she sleeps unsanctified by Church rites or priestly prayers. May the sweetest wild-flowers bloom around her! May her soul rest in the perfect joy and peace of heaven!

Though I sometimes saw a scowl on the face of the Indians whom I met, and whom I had sought to benefit before their evil passions had been aroused,

I was amused, and not displeased, by the following story, which was told me afterwards by one of the Crees.

Near my residence in those days was a very retired place, where both water and facilities for encampment are found. Without my knowing it, a band of Indians had hidden themselves there, awaiting the order for an outbreak. Day by day, from the rising ground, they watched me in my garden, and discussed what they should do with me when the massacre began ; and it was kindly decided that they would not meddle with the little white-robed priest, for I had not been bad to the Indian ; but as for my mare, they might take her if they should be pressed for horses. At that time several Indian dogs prowled around at night-time, and this caused some remark. Excepting this sign, which was soon forgotten, there was no evidence that an Indian encampment was so near. The Indian can be very secret in his ways. As for the danger, I had, both at the time and afterwards, many proofs that it was very real; even the Indian children had decided what particular plunder they intended to appropriate ; and they practised their bows and arrows in order to join in the fray. It was settled what families should be clubbed, in order to save the expense of powder and shot; and what women should be taken captive, and whose particular tent these fair ones were to adorn. I do not say that there were no bands loyal to the Government ; but there were certainly very few in which there was no disaffection, and a very great pressure was put upon them all to throw off their allegiance. The chief things that prevented the open revolt of all the bands were the influence of the Churches and the prompt action of the military authorities.

CHAPTER XV.

CHARACTERISTICS OF THE INDIANS—MR. EVANS: HIS WORK, MISTAKE, AND PERSECUTION.

I N addition to the foregoing observations respecting the Indian character and the Indian ways,
a few facts may be acceptable. Here, as everywhere, we shall find a great variety of characters.
Some Indians are very degraded—equal in degradation to any human beings that can be found anywhere ; if, indeed, such Indians can be called human
beings at all. Soon after my settlement in the
North-West, a man was brought in from the Peace
River district, and tried at Fort Saskatchewan, who
was a most horrible cannibal. It was proved that
he had killed and eaten his wife, her mother, and
three of his children. He was hung at Fort Saskatchewan, but seemed altogether indifferent to his
fate. Another man, in the midst of the settlement,
deliberately stabbed his wife, and, having paid blood-
money to her relatives, considered that he had com-
mitted no crime. This Eastern idea is very common
among the Indians of North America. In certain
ways they were very honest. Years ago you might

travel anywhere on the plains, and your property would be respected. Hudson Bay stores might be safely left unlocked, and no one would steal from them. If powder and shot were taken from a store in the absence of a keeper, the full value of skins would be left behind for payment, and at proper times full explanations would be made. A written communication was very sacred, and would be faithfully delivered at any distance. In some other matters their ideas of right and wrong were very peculiar, as I found in my business transactions with them. When I built my first shanty, as it was a very small place, and the winter was close at hand, I bought twelve cowhides from a butcher, and sent them to an Indian woman to be dressed. They had cost me twelve dollars. I thought that, if they were nailed to the log walls, they would help to keep the frost out, and make the shanty comfortable. When I supposed the hides were dressed, I went to the tent door, and asked for them in my best Cree, expecting to receive them, when the woman coolly told me I could not have them. On pressing for an explanation, I was informed that the skins had been dressed, but as she had no tea or tobacco, they had been cut up into strips, and sold at the Hudson Bay stores for shagganappi — no doubt to the amusement of the gentleman behind the counter, whose idea of honesty could not have been very exalted.

Although the Indian is not cleanly in his personal habits, the traveller may see everywhere that he has had his Turkish bath. Willow sticks are bent into the ground, and covered closely, and, by heated stones, hot vapour is produced sufficient to cause free perspiration. Then the bather takes a plunge into the snow, or into very cold water, just as his betters do in Europe, only in a more simple and natural way. In some parts a dog-feast is a great event, as it is also in China and among the Mongolians.

It is well known that the Indian is a great ' swell,' or ' dandy,' with his beadwork and paint. There are learned men in Europe, and scientific ethnologists, who make the native American to be indigenous to the soil, and class him as a distinct type of the human race, calling him the ' red man.' But, in twenty years' travel, I have never seen such a man. When the 'Red Indian' has his paint washed off, and lives in a house, his colour is tawny, and identical with the colour of the Mongolian. Here, as in other matters, superficial observation has led even educated men to form theories that can be corrected only with difficulty, though they are not based on well-attested facts.

I have often been surprised at the native intelligence and refinement which are found on these plains, among persons who are classed as Indians. It was my custom, during many years, to spend weeks at a time at Saddle Lake, which was more than a hundred miles from Edmonton Fort. In the evening the chief called the people together into his tent for prayers. When these were over, the chief men would retire, at my invitation, to the public lodge, and there, being seated in a circle, with their pipes lighted, at the expense of the missionary, who himself neither smoked nor used tobacco, the work of the evening would begin, and it would last far into the night, and even till the early morning. The conversation would be somewhat as follows :

'Friends, I am glad to meet you again. You remember what I have said before ; now ask me frankly whatever is in your minds.'

Then there would be silence for a minute or two, for it is part of the dignity of the Indian never to be in a hurry. Then the reply would be made, amid signs of general assent:

'We also are glad to meet you here ; it is very good of you to come so far to teach us the things of religion ; we are poor people, and very few care about us.'

Then silence.

'As you are so kind, we would like to ask you some questions. Please tell us what is the Christian religion ?'

'It is the religion which Jesus Christ lived and taught, in the Holy Land, eighteen hundred years ago, of which the New Testament gives us an account. You can most of you read the New Testament in Cree.'

'Yes, but we want a wise teacher to explain things to us. We are ignorant, and know nothing.'

'God, the Great Spirit, knows that, and it is to such as you He sends His Word, or Gospel, and

His Church, in order to lead you in the heavenly way.'

Sounds of assent.

'Pray tell us where the Christian religion came from.'

Now the missionary must be very careful, so he replies :

' This form of it which I bring to you comes from England (not from Rome), and the wise men of the Church teach, that the English Church is a branch of the true Christian religion, which in very early times was planted in England from Jerusalem, where the religion first arose as the Mother Church.'

' Not from Rome, then ?'

' No, not from Rome at first, although the Roman is a very ancient form of the Christian religion ; but it got changed very much, and both became closely connected in the Middle Ages, until the period of the Great Reformation.'

Silence for several minutes, while more tobacco is prepared for the pipes.

' Kindly tell us what a Christian man ought to believe.'

' He must believe the Creeds, which we rehearse every Sunday and whenever we worship, and this is all explained more fully in the Bible, and in the sermons preached by the clergymen.'

' What shall a Christian man do ?'

' A Christian man must keep the Commandments ; he must love God and man, and learn to walk all his days in the heavenly way. The Saviour established in His Church certain rites and ordinances ; through the observance of these we may receive help and grace, so as to be enabled to do His will.'

'Some of us are not Christian Indians, and we do not like to leave the way of our fathers. They were often good men, and taught us to fear and serve the good Spirit, and we do not like to leave the way they taught us. The Christian religion, you say, teaches us to honour our parents.'

'You do well to reverence your ancestors, and to follow their ways in all that is good and true. But you say that they were often wise, and lived according to their light; then, if a brighter light had come to them, they would have received it, and tried to live it ; so now, if they could speak, and their voices could be heard in this tent, they would say, " This word you hear is better light than we had, and if we had heard it we would have believed. Children ! follow the highest wisdom, and this the Christian religion teaches. We would embrace that religion were we living in the world now." '

In no part of the world could a teacher of religion be more wisely questioned, or in so nice a way ; but the fact must not be forgotten, that we were on the prairies of North America, and in an Indian tent, surrounded by uncivilized people who are conscious of their ignorance. Many of these people read and write the Cree character, as it is called, with much ease. When the language is known, a few weeks' practice suffices to make it familiar to the learner. The Cree language is regular in its formations, and the form of writing it is stenographic. For some time I wondered from whom it was derived, but no one whom I knew could tell me. At last I discovered that a Mr. Evans, a Wesleyan missionary in these territories, was its originator. He had in former days been a printer and reporter in England, so he made blocks, and set up types, and with great difficulty printed his little books for the Indians, and taught them to read his method of writing Cree. It was, in fact, the ordinary shorthand, a little changed, which was in common use fifty years ago, and it is admirably adapted for its purpose, with its affixes, and suffixes, and stem-writing. Many men have become notable for a less useful work than this, and I cannot but hold Mr. Evans' name in much honour. This good missionary is a type of the devoted men who for many years have sacrificed themselves on these plains, but who are scarcely remembered by those who reap the harvest of their toils. Mr. John McLean, in his ' Notes of a Twenty-five Years' Service in the Hudson Bay Territory,' says : ' The Rev. Mr. Evans, a man no less remarkable for genuine piety than for energy and decision of character, had been present at several of the annual meetings of the Indians at Manitonlin Island, and he felt his sympathy deeply awakened by the sight of their degradation and spiritual destitution. While thus affected he received an invitation from the American Episcopal Methodists to go as a missionary to the Indians resident in the Union. Feeling, however, that his services were rather due

to his fellow-subjects, he resolved to devote his
labours and life to the tribes residing in the Hudson
Bay Territory. Having made known his intentions
to the Canada Conference, he, together with Messrs.
Thomas Hurlburt and Peter Jacobs, was by them
appointed a missionary, and at their charges sent
to that territory. No application was made to the
company, and neither encouragement nor support
was expected from them. Mr. Evans and his
brother missionaries began their operations by raising
with their own hands a house at the Pic, themselves
cutting and hauling the timber on the ice. They
obtained, indeed, a temporary lodging at Fort
Michipicoton; and they not only found their own
provisions, but also materially increased the comforts
of the establishment by their success in fishing and
hunting. Late in the fall, accompanied by two
Indian boys in a small canoe, Mr. Evans made a
voyage to Sault St. Marie for provisions. On this
expedition, which was rendered doubly hazardous
by the lateness of the season and the inexperience
of his companions, he more than once narrowly
escaped being lost.

'Returning next season to Canada for his family,
he met Sir G. Simpson on Lake Superior. Having
learned that the mission was already established,
and likely to succeed, Sir George received him with
the utmost urbanity, treating him not only with
kindness, but even with distinction. He expressed
the highest satisfaction at the establishment of the
mission, promised him his utmost support, and at

length proposed an arrangement which, however auspicious for the infant mission, was ultimately found to be very prejudicial to it.

' The caution of Mr. Evans was completely lulled asleep by the apparent kindness of the Governor, and the hearty warmth with which he seemed to enter into his views. Sir George proposed that missionaries should hold the same rank, and receive the same allowance, as the wintering partners or commissioned officers, and that canoes and other means of conveyance should be furnished to the missionaries for their expeditions. It did not seem unreasonable to stipulate that, in return for these substantial benefits, they should do or say nothing prejudicial to the company's interests, either among the natives or in their reports to the Conference in England, to whose jurisdiction the mission was transferred. The great evil of this arrangement was, that the missionaries, instead of being the servants of God, and accountable to Him alone, became the servants of the Hudson Bay Company, and dependent on and amenable to them. The committee were, of course, to be the sole judges of what was or was not prejudicial to their interests. Still, it is impossible to blame very severely either Mr. Evans or the Conference for accepting offers which were apparently so advantageous, or even for con-senting to certain restrictions in publishing their reports. With the assistance and co-operation of the company, great good might be effected ; with the hostility of a corporation which was all but omnipotent within its own domain and among the Indians, the post might not be tenable.

'For some time matters went on smoothly. By the indefatigable exertions of Mr. Evans and his fellow-workers, aided also by Mrs. Evans, who devoted much of her time and labour to the instruction of the females, a great reformation was effected in the habits and morals of the Indians. But Mr. Evans soon perceived that without books printed in the Indian language little permanent good would be realized; he therefore wrote to the London Conference to send him a printing-press and types, with characters of a simple phonetic kind, which he had himself invented, and of which he gave them a copy. The press was procured without delay, but was detained in London by the Governor and committee; and though they were again and again petitioned to forward it, they flatly refused. Mr. Evans, however, was not a man to be turned aside from his purpose. With his characteristic energy, he set to work, and, having invented an alphabet of a more simple kind, he with his penknife cut the types, and formed the letters from musket bullets; then he constructed a rude sort of press, and, aided by Mrs. Evans as a compositor, he at length succeeded in printing prayers, and hymns, and passages of Scripture for the use of the Indians. Finding their object in detaining the press thus baffled, the Governor and committee deemed it expedient to forward it, but with the express stipulation that everything printed should be sent to the commander of the post as censor, before it was published among the Indians. This was among the first causes of distrust and dissatisfaction.

'Not long after, finding that the missions he had hitherto superintended were in such a state of progress that he might safely leave them to the care of his fellow-labourers, Mr. Evans resolved to proceed to Athabasca, and establish a mission there. Having gone, as usual, to the commander of the post to obtain the necessary provision, and a canoe and boatmen, he was received with unusual coldness. He asked for provisions, none could be given; he offered to purchase them, the commander refused to sell him any; he begged a canoe, it was denied him; and finally, when he entreated that, if he should be able to procure these necessaries elsewhere, he might at least be allowed to take a couple of men to assist him on the voyage, he was answered that none would be allowed to go on that service. Deeply grieved, but nothing daunted, Mr. Evans procured these necessaries from private resources, and proceeded on the voyage. But a sad calamity put a stop to it. In handing his gun to the interpreter, it accidentally went off, and the charge lodging in the interpreter's breast, it killed him instantaneously. Mr. Evans was thus compelled to return, in a state of mind bordering on distraction. His zeal and piety promised the best results to the spiritual and eternal interests of his Indian brethren. His talents, energy, and fertility of resource, which seemed to rise with every obstacle, had the happiest effects on their temporal

well-being; and his mild and winning manners en-
deared him to all the Indians. But his useful and
honourable career was now drawing to a close. The
mournful accident already alluded to had affected
his health, and he had received his death-blow.

'Yet, obnoxious as he had become to the company, and formidable to their interests as they
might deem one of his talents and indomitable
resolution to be, the final blow was not struck by
them. It was dealt by a false brother—by one who
had eaten of his bread, by a familiar friend with
whom he had taken sweet counsel. Charges affect-
ing his character, both as a man and as a minister,
of the foulest and blackest kind, were transmitted to
the Conference by a brother missionary. To answer
these charges, which were as false as they were foul,
he was compelled to leave the churches which he
had planted and watered, to bid adieu to the people
whose salvation had been for years the sole object of
his life, and to undertake a voyage of five thousand
miles, in order to appear before his brethren as a
criminal.

'As a criminal, indeed, he was received; yet, after
an investigation which was begun and carried on in
no very friendly spirit to him, the truth prevailed.
He was declared innocent, and the right hand of
fellowship was again extended to him. He made a
short tour through England, and was everywhere
received with respect, and affection, and sympathy.
But anxiety, and grief, and shame had done their
work. Scarcely three weeks had passed by, when

one evening he was visiting, with Mrs. Evans, in
the family of a friend. He seemed to have recovered
much of his wonted cheerfulness, but late in the
evening Mrs. Evans, who had retired for a few
minutes, was suddenly summoned back to the room,
only to see her husband pass away into that land
where " the wicked cease from troubling." The
cause of his death was an affection of the heart.
And that man—the slanderer, the murderer of this
martyred missionary—what punishment was inflicted
on him? He is to this day unpunished. He yet lives
in the Hudson Bay Territory, the disgrace and the
opprobrium of his profession and his Church.'

This story is given as related by another person,
because Mr. McLean was acquainted with the circumstances, and I was anxious to keep in the public
memory so remarkable a benefactor of the Indians
and half-races of the Hudson Bay Territory. His
experience may very possibly be repeated even in
these later times. It is a standing danger in the
way of even the noblest and bravest missionary.
The more conscientious and self-sacrificing he may
be, the greater is the danger of his being misunderstood, misrepresented, maligned, and persecuted.
A few years ago there was no baseness that would
fail to find its agents close at hand, and an apostle
of ancient days would easily have found his cross,
and a shameful martyrdom. I was especially interested in reading this account of Mr. Evans,
inasmuch as, twenty-five years ago, before there was
much travel on the beautiful Muskoka Lakes, I fell

in with two fellow-travellers, in crossing a portage
between Rosseau Lake and Muskoka Lake, and one
of them was a well-dressed Indian, speaking correct
English; but he was intoxicated, and was carrying
liquor with him. He could not have been more vile
in his behaviour, and he volunteered to tell us his
name and his former profession, and declared that,
on his visit to England, he had been introduced to
the Queen as an Indian missionary from the Hudson
Bay Territories. I shall never forget the disgust
which I felt and expressed, although we were in a
lonely region, and an accident of shooting or stab-
bing might easily have occurred. This creature was
the vile Judas who had been the agent of Mr.
Evans' martyrdom—but what an agent to be used
in such a business!

A great deal has been said about the *trading* of
missionaries in these territories, and their traffic in
furs in the days when fur was abundant; much of
what was said arose from jealousy, lest the trade
should be diverted from the hands that held it.
The reports were rather preventive than real, and
any apparent liberality of a fur company might thus
be accounted for. Long ago a missionary had no
means of sending any fur out of the country, and
every skin he possessed would be well known at
the forts. The missionary simply could not trade
until most of the fur was exhausted and the country
was opened up to the 'free traders,' whose advent
was of quite a late date—say about 1870. If a
missionary visited an encampment at a distance

8—2

from his residence, and took any provisions with
him for personal use, such as flour, tea, or sugar,
the Indians would think him very mean if he refused
to part with a portion to women or sick people
who required their use, and were far from the forts,
where they could be obtained and exchanged for
furs ; and yet if the missionary, with his limited
means, had done what the traders did, and given
kind for kind, he would have been branded as a
trader who, while professing to be seeking the
spiritual good of the Indians, was making himself
rich at the expense of his position. Missionary
societies would have heard the garbled story, and
most likely would have recalled him as unworthy
of his profession. Flour worth five pounds a bag,
and tea five shillings a pound, must be given away,
and the skins must be left behind for the fur trader,
who made it his business to collect furs, and who
had no religious profession to hinder his making a
large profit. During a course of twenty years I
have not even received a rabbit-skin from an Indian,
to say nothing of more valuable furs. Two buffalo
robes were presented to me, one by a gentleman of
the Mounted Police Force, and another as the
Christmas-gift of my people at All Saints', Edmonton.
When I wanted fur robes for my journeys, I went
to the fort, and paid Montreal prices for buffalo
robes of second and third-rate quality, which were
the only ones procurable. Every valuable robe
was precious, and sent away to Montreal to
enhance the reputation of the local agent for in-

dustry in forwarding the best skins to the front markets.

Criticism on missionaries has often been unfair, and utterly unworthy of generous minds, who might look with kindly eye upon even the most crack-brained enthusiasts, in consideration of good intention, and the life of self-sacrifice which their work requires.

CHAPTER XVI.

LAND RIGHTS OF FIRST SETTLERS.

TO one who was accustomed in early life to the quiet orderliness and the almost cast-iron customs and habits of English life, the changes which I have observed here in Edmonton during the last twenty years are very interesting. Not far away from me now the Indians are just leaving off making flints for their arrow-heads, and bushels of these flints may be picked up on the old camping-grounds. When I began my work, the soil of my garden had never before been cultivated; it was virgin soil, fresh from the hands of the Creator. Through long centuries the same grass had flowered and cast its seed; and the wild-roses summer by summer had bloomed, and thrown around their fragrance. The willow-bushes had waved their branches, unmolested by the hand of man, for thousands of years. But now the land has been broken up, and the spade, the hoe, and the plough are in use. Fresh seeds are sown, both for use and for ornament, and trees are brought from afar which revive old memories, the planter hoping they will take kindly to the new soil and thrive in the new surroundings; and this they sometimes, but not always, do.

It seems as if no one country could be altogether like another; even in aspect it must vary, and show certain differences. The sentiments and the thoughts of human beings are influenced and moulded by fresh conditions, and consequently much of the old remains, while the new is not quite new. Old and new commingle so as to produce fresh forms of civilization, even when new lands are inhabited by ancient or imported races. The freshness there is in the commonest things fills the mind with uncertainty, and yet with an unlimited hopefulness. We do not know what is about to happen when we sow the seed or plant the trees; but we feel that anything is possible in new lands, and that any day great discoveries may be made which may prove of the highest importance to the world. We bore for oil, we search for gold, we open coal-mines, full of expectation, and such enterprises consciously or unconsciously mould our inner thought and feeling. We have nothing old to fall back upon; we must make all things new, since the old will not fit the new circumstances.

At first, even if we had an abundance of money, it would be out of place to build palaces; log-houses fit the passing conditions, and we build and plant for awhile, living as close as possible to Nature. By-and-by we decide to erect permanent dwellings, when Nature is fairly conquered and life humanized;

but everything must come in its proper place and time. Our politic relations grow in a similar way. First we have the district meeting, which is to arrange about our roads, and our schools, and the other primitive wants of the neighbourhood. Then we take in the township, the county, and the province. These are joined to an older or larger province, and then these provinces unite to send representatives to a general Parliament, which reacts on us by ensuring social order, and making laws which will supplement our local institutions, and weld us together as one responsible people.

A careful observer is struck with the naturalness of these arrangements. They are the working out of conditions which require little statesmanship, only the most plodding common-sense. Confederation is the simple hanging together of a chain of provinces which are similar in climate and circumstances, without the inward union out of which real nationalities grow. To make a people one, some great common idea and sentiment must be cherished, which will give them a common life, that is sure to demand organization.

At present the question arises, as we think of the future of Canada, Where is the uniting principle that will make us a real nation ? Is it to be found in religion ? That is the first bond of nations. Alas ! we are divided into a hundred jarring sects, and these conflict in every settlement, and village, and city throughout the land. Is the union one of politics ? All the provinces fight for their own hand, in

order to get their own men into power; and the
chief object, apart from personal ambition, is to
obtain grants of money from the general funds for
the local advantage of the districts. Is the uniting
principle loyalty to Great Britain? If England
would let the provinces do what they wish, and the
mother-country would bear the expense of empire
uncomplainingly, the feeling of loyalty to the Queen
might, in time of strain, hold the provinces together.
But distance from the centre of empire, differences
in circumstances which may easily occasion misunderstanding, and the self-sufficiency which is characteristic of young nations, will greatly try this loyalty to
England, as the basis and inspiration of Canadian
national unity.

The Divine Providence alone knows what will
make a nation of us; but we are now a people
full of confusion, and without either conscious aims
or a manifest destiny. Then, the changes that are
passing around us speak loudly of the first principles
of law and order. Here we have, for example, the
land question, which Nature herself is teaching us
and solving for us. Land is abundant, and it is of
no use or worth until it is occupied and cultivated—
until a man puts his labour into it, and lives a hard
life while he is preparing it for a crop. It is his
honest toil which makes the land his own. Even
the Indians are growing out of associated labour,
and taking up homesteads of their own. In a
neighbourly way one settler helps another, and
receives the labour back again. Men see plainly

enough that holding land in association, and working it together, would not be a just mode, or one that could be successful in husbandry. The growth of the Socialistic spirit in our new conditions of life is never even thought of as possible. The universal feeling is, that if a man wants land he must go on a piece set apart for him, and improve it by his own labour, and make an estate for himself and his family, on which he may live an independent life, and so form a part of a general voluntary society.

Socialism in land may be the dream of congested cities, and of mechanics in towns who toil hard for daily bread; but it will not lift its head in such countries as North-West Canada, where land is abundant, and the toil of cultivating it is great. Why does not the Socialist take up his common right with us? We will not hinder him; but if after ten years' experience he remains Socialist, and wishes to put his theory on land into practice, he will find himself the butt of universal laughter, and simple common-sense will cover him with ridicule.

The notions which cause so much commotion in Europe, if they were tested in our new conditions, where they would have fair play, and could be tried even by those who believe in them, would soon demonstrate themselves, and show their inutility for the production of human prosperity and happiness. Honest labour alone will make true wealth, and land is yet abundant in God's great world, where all could be fed and clothed if the Divine laws were but

efficiently carried out. Crude notions and intellectual dreams cannot cheat Nature. She placidly lets
her children try their whims, but behind her hand is
surely hid her rod for punishment, when those whims
are false, however decorated they may be with the
names of wisdom and philosophy.

What can be a greater folly in these new countries
than the idea of placing the chief national taxation
on the land, in order that it may bear the chief
burden of the State? We are in the process of
beginning to exist; our wealth has to be made. Our
anxiety at first is how to live at all. To take up
land, and to work it, is to begin the fight for bread,
and very often it is a life-and-death struggle for
many long years. Is it fair, or right, or even
prudent, to 'kill the goose that lays the golden
egg'? What are manufactures, and merchants,
and professions, without agriculture as a thriving
industry? Absolutely nothing. The land is the
mother who feeds them all. Who turned our
prairies into farms, and gave them value? The
men who rescued the soil and made it useful. No
Government did it; no merchant or manufacturer
did it. Who, then, can ever claim, on any ground
of justice, the right to oppress this interest? or, even
on State-social theories, to take the land from its
owners for some supposed national good? The land
is, with us, pre-eminently *real estate*, and it is given,
at first hand, by Heaven to the first cultivator, who
has a title which is as ancient as the title to the
Garden of Eden. For 'the Lord God took the man,

and put him into the Garden of Eden, to dress it and to keep it.'

This reasoning does not apply to the land which is given away, and held, by the favour of men in power, for mere speculative purposes. Such land is to be sold again when the labour of the husbandman has made it valuable in the market. This misuse of land, this stealing of God's domain from the poor and the landless, is a grievous sin and iniquity, which will cry to heaven for vengeance on the guilty and those who rob God. Such speculation in public lands anywhere is the seed of revolutions that almost justify the basest passions and the most universal anarchy. No crime has been more common than this among public men throughout the American Continent. Extreme Socialists and Nihilists fasten their eyes on riches gathered in such ways, and they forget the self-sacrifice and toil of the many in their disgust at the riches of the few and the unscrupulous. They are not in the mood to remember the wisdom of the householder, who said of the wheat and the tares, ' Let both grow together until the harvest, and in the time of harvest I will say to the reapers, Gather ye together first the tares, and bind them in bundles to burn them ; but gather the wheat into my barn.'

Among other changes taking place, there is the growth of villages and towns. But yesterday the land was all solitude, and now on all sides arise centres of business which, to avoid offence, must be gravely designated cities. Some enterprising persons get land surveyed into small lots; advertise the place as the centre of everything and everywhere; a store is set up, a hotel, a room for a meeting-place, a blacksmith's shop, and a church for every denomination; and if fortune favour the audacity, the place grows for a time, lots are bought and sold, until a rush takes place to see what can be 'made,' and then all sorts of people congregate, and endeavour to outwit one another. Often, in these incipient towns, it is as well not to inquire particularly what the idea and practice of the moralities are. It is not long ago since it was considered a witticism worthy of laughter to exclaim: 'The Almighty has not got so far as this yet'—a saying that is suggestive to a wise and thoughtful man of the condition of things if all churches and religious institutions were absent, or if the culture of the sense of God in the human soul were neglected as a basis of civilization. The missionary comes face to face, in a very vivid manner, with the fact that without religion civilization could not exist. Mankind, especially the so-called civilized humanity, would quickly degenerate into mere animal life, and the dwelling-places of men would become dens of misery by reason of the lawlessness of their greed, and of their other base passions. By-and-by this rowdyism gives way to a better condition of things, as people of more settled habits find their way into a new district; but it is always a long time before the intense restlessness of these populations is conquered, and that spirit of reverence and repose

comes which alone forms a proper basis for the
higher intellectual and religious life. It is true that
we have a certain surface intelligence and sharpness
in our new communities, but learning, in any real
sense, is seldom met with. We cannot appreciate it,
and it is generally looked upon as a useless incum-
brance. The question is often asked, What use is
it? will it bring money? Education comprises
simply arithmetic, writing a fair hand, the elements
of grammar, and a smattering of history, compiled
by almost anybody who can get his books introduced
into the public schools; but the idea of correct
thinking, the discipline of mind, or body, or spirit,
in order that the purposes of life may be wisely
fulfilled, is almost nowhere found; the one idea is to
get on, to make an appearance, to have a good time
—in a word, to enjoy the physical life to its utmost.
In our state of society a man who reads, and thinks,
and lives a life of contemplation, who has an ideal of
any kind that he wishes to realize, is likely to be
regarded as a crank, or a very peculiar person; and
however gentle in manner he may be, he is almost
always disliked, and if he should have the slightest independence of spirit, he will soon be even hated. Such
men sometimes come and look on things for awhile,
but then quickly fly away to other climes where they
may be at rest. Yet these are the men we so greatly
need, as an influence to quicken us to higher things,
and to show us what civilization really is. Men may
be contented with themselves, because they know no
better, or they may have lost their sense of the value

of deep thought and feeling, and then the scholar, the poet, the artist, the cultivated teacher of religion, are necessary, and all the more necessary in that at first they are so little valued and welcomed.

It is not long since I was on a visit to a distant part of my mission, and was receiving the hospitality of a retired trader. He was an old man, and had lived for years in the Mackenzie River district, seeing little of human life, and only reading of it in books and newspapers. He had, however, thought a good deal, and the desire possessed him to settle where there were more people, so that in his old age he might gather around him a few rays of civilization, and some of the blessings it should bring. Looking earnestly in my face, he said: ' May I ask you a question ? Is that civilization which I see when I go into —— ?' He had not realized his ideal; he was simply shocked to find ' white men' contented with a condition of morals and manners that was in no way better than could be found around mission-stations in the most distant settlements. It is this kind of civilization which does such great harm in these districts among the natives of the country. They first look on with surprise and revulsion, then they imitate, and quickly and wildly rush on to their own utter extinction.

For sixteen years, in a country as large as England, while these changes were taking place, I was the only clergyman of the Church of England. I had to cover this ground, and to travel everywhere alone, as I could not afford a servant. Alone I crossed the rivers, slept at night wherever I could, and often simply under the trees, and miles away from any human being. Alone I attended to my horse, and prepared my meals. If people were sick they sent for me. If children were to be baptized, or parties wanted to be married, I had to go anywhere for the service. Now, in 1895, in a few chief centres, there are other clergymen carrying on the work, and doing their best to grapple with the difficulties of a large and very mixed immigration. I am supposed to be retired, after twenty years of this real missionary work, to a parish eight miles square, where I can do the duties of a country priest, and comfort myself with the thought that I belong to the class of country clergymen who, like Herbert and Keble, are the glory of the Church of England.

Once I broke down when on a journey by a lonely road. I was trying to repair a broken screw of my conveyance, when there came along four persons. One was an American, travelling to view the country; the others knew me well, and with great readiness gave me their assistance in repairing the accident. The American, observing the manner of my native friends, came up to me, and in his friendly fashion said : ' Sir, may I ask who you are, and what is your station in the Church ? Are you Archdeacon, Bishop, or what ?' Not expecting these questions, I could only reply : ' No ; I am none of these, and I have no ambition for such offices. I have only wished for many years to be the good

Samaritan of this whole country-side.'   With a
bright light in his eyes the American answered :
' Thank you, sir, that will do,' and went on his way.
This reply of mine was quite unpremeditated, but
on full reflection I am quite contented with it.   Still,
as ever, the lowliest service is the highest in the
Church of Him who came ' not to be ministered unto
but to minister, and to give His life a ransom for
many.'

CHAPTER XVII.

DIFFICULTIES OF CHURCH WORK.

MISSIONARY work in this far North-West has three branches. There is the Indian work, the town work, and the work of the travelling missionary among the settlers. As we are situated now, the Indian work is the easiest, and the most independent and agreeable. In this case the missionary has his work close at hand; the Government and the missionary societies help him, and benevolent persons of various kinds render him assistance. There need be no travelling, nor much wear and tear either of body or of mind. A missionary at an Indian mission station now is not much to be pitied; his accommodation is excellent, his living is good, he has his services close at hand, his work claims sympathy and attention, and these to a great extent he gains. I would sooner be engaged in this work, in the Saskatchewan and Alberta districts, than in any other kind of work, had I my choice and did circumstances allow me to choose. As I view it, the Indian work includes the mission to the half-race, which cannot now be wisely separated from it.

ST. MARY'S PRO-CATHEDRAL, PRINCE ALBERT, NORTH-WEST TERRITORIES.

To face page 130.

While I write, an eminent Roman Catholic missionary of this country is endeavouring to induce the Canadian Government to give reserves of land for the accommodation of the Indians. I do not anticipate much good result from such an arrangement. Already they have received 'scrip' for special lands, but these have at last fallen into the hands of traders. The half-race and the Indian are so mixed that no one can separate them; and the majority on the reserves and in the schools are half-race rather than Indian. Now that they are all learning to speak English, some will rise in the social scale, and the others will quickly pass away. Neither the half-race question nor the Indian question can be dealt with in any permanent way. From a variety of causes these questions are fast solving themselves, and they had better work out their manifest destiny. Real kindness would help these people to cheap schools, and to secure fitting stipends for their clergy —for the half-breeds usually gather themselves into communities. In other ways they could be encouraged to independence and self-help, and this would be far better than plunging them into full pauperism.

Our next missionary work is the work of the Church in the towns. There are no villages here; they are all either towns or cities. Probably our town work is like that which has to be done in all our colonies where the circumstances are similar. This work is as much Congregationalism as it can be under a bishopric. The people who form the congregations are new to one another. They manage their affairs by committees; and, as they provide the minister's stipend, they are the masters of the situation, and they virtually control both the priest and the bishop. The Australian colonist farmer said to his bishop, 'Yes, you may send the minister; but if we don't like un we won't pay un.' Considering the various tastes and opinions of these new communities whose members are gathered from everywhere, it would be a miracle if any clergyman suited them all equally well.

In large cities, here as elsewhere, congregations are formed of separate classes, to suit the views of the classes; but it cannot be so in the small towns. They all must meet in one church-building, and there are sure to be differences of opinion amongst them. The Church work of the small towns is, therefore, a very difficult matter, whether the clergyman be what is known as high, or low, or broad Church, or whether he is no Churchman at all. He may be ever so sincere and prudent, and yet he may give offence if he turn to the east in the Creed, or if he does not turn; if the altar have a cross, or if a cross be absent; if he wear coloured stoles, or only a black one. He will be too poetical in his preaching for one person, and too dry for another; too doctrinal for some folk, and not doctrinal enough for other folk. As a rule, he must not be more than thirty-five years of age, or he is likely to be 'an old man'; and then, whatever may be the value of his services, 'he ought to be superannuated'—of course, at somebody else's expense. The younger he is, the better for him; the more handsome he is, the more charming, especially as a large portion of his stipend is usually raised by 'The Ladies' Aid Society.' It is always best to keep popular with them, as otherwise the necessary amount may not be forthcoming. This 'Ladies' Aid Society' can often 'wag the dog,' priest, bishop, and all, except the business men to whom the clergyman may be indebted.

Experience goes for very little; modesty wins no laurels, and it is not usually classed with learning and ability. Besides, the people composing these small town congregations are often roamers; they seldom stay long in one place, and a year or two provides quite another set of worshippers, and all the work has to be begun again. Generally, too, assistance is difficult to get in carrying on the Sunday-schools and other enterprises, except those which cater for the popular amusement. Helpers for these are usually ready, if an appeal be duly made to their self-esteem.

In raising funds for Church work, what strange schemes are set on foot! Dances, concerts, bazaars, meals sold on racecourses; these things would astonish the old saints and martyrs, who planted the Cross in altogether different ways in those ignorant times and dark ages—the times 'before our modern enlightenment.' They gave their lives, and all they had, in a holy sacrifice, as history tells; but we offer our amusements, and call these our self-sacrifice. In true self-sacrifice our people are apt to be very deficient; they are not often willing

givers, either of time or money, for their church, so
that a very heavy burden is laid upon the minister
in carrying on the services, and the affairs of the
congregation, in these small places. The secret of
this want of zeal arises from deficient Churchman-
ship. It seems almost impossible for Church ideas
to take root and thrive in our new colonies. The
people have no historic sense. There is nothing in
which it can grow. Their notions are of to-day, or
at most of yesterday ; their hope and thought are in
the future ; their dreams are of coming times. So
the Church of England is at a disadvantage. Her
ideas and methods are not new ; they are ancient :
what, therefore, have they to do with young America ?
True, this may be a passing phase of human feeling, but
it applies to our new towns, and it is of these that we
are now speaking. There is need of patient sowing
and planting, but such quiet forms of work are at a
discount. No one in these places is likely to believe
in any work which does not advertise itself by noise
and blare of trumpets ; and without these ' whoever
hears of the minister ?'—' he is nowhere,' 'the Church
and the clergyman are failures,' and subscriptions
are not paid. Faithful spiritual work may be readily
trampled down by the destructive feet of a thought-
less multitude.

The Church in new settlements may also suffer
from the looseness of her membership. Her spirit is
not exclusive, and she admits all comers into her
fold ; but this weakens the Church in her special
character and work. If people are nominal Church-

men, without Church ideas and convictions, they are
simply captured by the more earnest spirit that is in
the sects around them, and the 'liberality' of these
nominal Churchmen is so great, that they will give
money and help to other bodies, for the sake of their
business connections and social influence, and fail
adequately to support their own Church. Especially
are they deficient in the moral courage that is necessary in order to defend their Church from the attacks
and misrepresentations of the sects around them ;
and of these, in our state of society, there is always
an abundance. In a Church, as in an army, it is
not the numbers but the discipline of the men that
makes a general successful. Insubordination, re-
fractoriness, want of sympathy with the objects of
the war, will cause the failure of the best general,
because, in that case, he has to fight his army as
well as his enemy.

Writing as a clergyman who has watched the
state of the Church of England in Canada, and in
the new towns that are springing up in the North-
West territories, I cannot but express my conviction
that this is a chief cause of the general unrest of our
clergy. They are, as a rule, inadequately supported
by their people, not only in money, but in that
spiritual and intellectual sympathy which so materially helps to produce and to sustain a strong and
successful ministry.

At one time I experienced something of this
crooked spirit in one of the towns in which I had
planted the Church. I had great trouble at first in

laying the foundation, and then in building on it; but I took special care of the young people. Local circumstances were not favourable, and local influences were against us if we persisted in building on Church lines. Year by year, on the evening of Christmas Day, I gathered the children into the church, which was our only place of meeting. The children and the visitors crammed the church, and we had a splendid festival, and all seemed to be delighted with it. The other denomination had their festival on the same night, and came to me to ask me to change my evening, as the meetings would clash, and many of my people had promised to give them their assistance. They all knew that for several years previously I had held my festival on this particular evening, and wanted for it the help of the Churchpeople as a matter of course. I announced the festival as usual, and it succeeded, while the other failed; and then minister, wife, and others came to see what we were doing, but as the building was packed, and I had to manage everything, I could not receive visitors or pay any persons special attention. Besides this, in honour of the occasion, and to show respect to the children, who, although they were natives of the country, were nicely dressed, and on their best behaviour, I put on a special vestment, and wore a little cross, which I have often found helpful among the Indians on the plains when we were strangers. The business over, the ladies wished me good-night, and hoped that I would always use my gown, even in the ordinary Church services. I went to my Hermitage very weary, but very contented with the festival. A few days passed, and then I had to start on a journey of a hundred and twenty miles, in bitterly cold weather, to perform a marriage ceremony. On my way I called at the post-office, and there received the following communication :

'REV. AND DEAR SIR,

'From the friendship that has existed between us since I came to ——, I think it my duty to make you acquainted with the impression which your conduct lately, especially on Christmas evening, has made on your members and others. Several of them have spoken to me on the subject, and expressed themselves simply disgusted with your treatment of the Rev. Mr. H—— and his wife, who attended your festival ; and with your wearing conspicuously on a black gown a white cross.

'I fear your influence here is gone.

'Believe me, my dear sir,

'Yours truly,

'A. B——.

'P.S.—I have learned that a petition to the Bishop is being got up for your removal.

'To REV. DR. NEWTON.'

To this the following reply was sent :

'All Saints, *January.*

'MY DEAR SIR,

'Your letter of the 9th instant has just been received by me. I thank you for any kind expressions the letter contains: any other matters will be referred " home," with such explanations as circumstances may make necessary.

' Certainly no one desired to be rude to Mr. and Mrs. H——, nor do I think any rudeness was shown them by anybody at our Christmas festival.

' With kind regards, I am, as ever,

' Sincerely yours,

' WM. NEWTON.

' To A. B——, Esq.'

The petition was prepared, sent round, and signed by a few persons; but I heard nothing of it until a Roman Catholic gentleman asked me if I knew what became of it, and I said that I did not. He replied that the petition had been sent both to Methodists and Catholics to sign. He further said, ' It came to *me*, but I took care to place it where it will give no more trouble to anybody.'

Years afterwards, when changes had taken place, the writer of the foregoing letter took himself off to the Baptist congregation, where he doubtless felt more at home than in regulating the amount of ritual to be observed in the services of the Church of England.

But what a state of things is revealed in our Church, when persons of such opinions and feelings can have any influence in determining the methods of a clergyman's work, and this chiefly because of the necessity of considering the amount of their subscriptions.

CHAPTER XVIII.

I T remains to mention the third kind of missionary work in this far North-West, viz., mission work among settlers. The Indian work is on reserves. The town clergyman may or may not supply out-stations, but he has his chief work near his home. The mission to settlers is, in fact, a mission at large, and may cover immense distances, and only occasional services can be held in any one district. This has been my principal work for twenty-five years; for five years in Muskoka, and for twenty years in these North-West territories. It is a very difficult and trying work; for the people to whom I ministered are widely scattered, either singly or in small groups, over an area of some two hundred miles. At first there were no roads or bridges to help the traveller. There were no inns, or stopping places, and it would take a week, or even sometimes a month, to go the rounds before the missionary could return to his home again. On these rough roads fifty miles a day would be no unusual journey, and it had to be undertaken in any weather; in summer surrounded by mosquitoes and horse-flies; in spring and autumn wading through mud and pools of water; and in the winter in the bitter cold, with the thermometer measuring 30, 40, and even more, degrees of frost. The work to be done includes the usual services of the church, the baptizing of children, the administration of the sacraments, and the visitation of the aged and the sick. When the night comes on, if the missionary is fortunate, he may sit beside the stove, either with the solitary settler or with an isolated family, and converse with a sympathy and confidence that are seldom known in the busier world, on matters of interest and importance relating both to this world and to the next.

The missionary meets with very various individuals on his tours. Now, it is a wandering American settler—a man who has roamed almost everywhere, and seen the wildest forms of life, or, perhaps, has been with General Custer in his last fight with the Indians. Another is a miner, who may not have been in a place of worship for twenty years. Another is a native of the country, who has never seen the sea, and thinks Winnipeg to be the centre of the universe. Another sold out in Ontario, and wandered here to begin life anew in this land of the setting sun. Another is a young man of good birth and breeding, who has been brought up at Eton or at Rugby, and has taken an Oxford or Cambridge degree, who, through some misfortune, or folly, has been cast upon the wide world. Many are the confidences that I have heard from this class in the evening twilight, or in the deeper silence of the night; tales as strange as any romance over which women weep and grave men look sad. Or it may be that the hut set up in the wilderness contains, on its rough walls, the portraits of a father, and mother, and sisters, and younger brothers, who are far away in some picturesque rectory in England, or in the front parts of Canada, whose anxious sympathies follow their son or their brother in his struggles to make an independent home in these vast solitudes.

While engaged in this work it has often seemed to me to be equal in value to any that the Church can undertake. Nothing can be more like the work of Christ, ' who went about doing good,' and told us of the shepherd, and of his wandering in order to seek the one lost sheep, and of the angels rejoicing over the one that was saved.

The true missionary cannot, in this section of the mission-field, fully report his work : he can only guess how many miles he has travelled ; no description can efficiently picture his risks in travelling, the poor accommodation, the badly prepared food, the seeds of ill-health sown, and the weariness of the journeyings he has endured. Besides the general services at certain centres, the spiritual work done in silence is, in proportion to its effectiveness, that of which neither he nor others can properly speak ; it cannot be blazoned abroad ; it is often too sacred even for the religious magazines.

In time, however, some of his work will become

visible. In the most unlikely places villages spring up and settlements are formed, a few earnest people gather others together for worship, and the 'small things not despised' are the beginnings of Christian institutions which will be sure to grow in usefulness and influence with the centuries. To do this settlers' work well, as it should be done, a clergyman needs many qualities of a high order; he should be no make-shift man, no crude person who is fit for no other work, and therefore put to this, for certainly such agency will prove worse than useless, and will only bring contempt on the Church, and this receives fresh proof every day. A travelling missionary lives in the full light, and is observed close at hand. He is surrounded by no enclosure of dignity, his every action is noticed and spoken of freely; the way he sits at table; the manner and the extent of his eating and drinking; his most simple actions are interpreted according to the feeling cherished towards him, and the opinion that people have formed of his character. If he be ignorant, it cannot be hidden; if selfish, his services will be ineffective; if proud, or vain, he is not in a city where he may strut to his heart's content. Here, as there are no places where comedy is enacted, they will place the missionary on the stage of their social life, and cover him with ridicule, and include in the ridicule not the man only, but also the cause which he represents.

To be efficient as a travelling missionary, a man must be vigorous in body and in mind. He must, indeed, 'endure hardness, as a good soldier of Jesus Christ.' He must be indifferent to luxury, or even ordinary convenience, and he should be as simple in his habits as the Spartans were. He must give himself no airs, but be the gentleman always, in feeling, in thought, and in action. Courtesy must be as natural to him as breathing, and it must be shown in his dealings with all, even the humblest. It is well for him never to take offence, and never to notice intentional or unintentional rudeness. His work won't bear contention, and he is to be an example of the Christian graces. His passions must be kept under control, for never were there such glass houses as are to be found in the wilderness. Everything is known; men seem to think almost audibly, and impressions of conduct are most direct. The missionary had better not use tobacco inordinately, or take spirits with him; and I have found it best, even when very weary, not to accept them when offered. As he for days must live in very simple relationship with families, within very limited house accommodations, he needs to be careful and modest in his deportment, especially with womankind, and to cultivate pure-heartedness. Besides this he must be prudent in speech, careful not to repeat what he sees or hears in the houses he visits, and never to break any confidences that are reposed in him. In a word, the travelling missionary must be really a Christian man—devout, sympathetic, good—a lowly image of the Master, who was the greatest of all missionaries.

Nor are the purely intellectual qualities to be neglected. Such a missionary comes directly into contact with individuals who have seen and read a great deal, and the missionary must face all men and be useful to them all. Tennyson's Northern Farmer should never be able to say of him :

'An' I hallus comed to his chorch afore my Sally was dead,
An' eered un a bummin awaäy loike a buzzard-clock ower my yead.'

He has no opportunity for 'bumming away.' Conversations of all kinds directly appeal to him on level ground ; and he must wisely give and take; keep his mind clear, and see that his knowledge ripens into wisdom. This will necessitate previous culture, wide reading, observation of human life, and habits of thoughtful meditation. How often on my visits I have seen the face lighted with a smile, as the solitary settler has filled his pipe, and prepared to converse with his friend and clergyman, who has put aside all formalities for the occasion. The beginning is usually :

' Sir, if you will be so kind I should like to ask you a question.'

' Yes ; what is it ?' is the reply.

The question may be on church history, or on some passage of Holy Scripture ; or the man has been reading Huxley or Emerson, or he requires light on the relation of this life to the life beyond, or a thousand other things. The missionary is there in order that under the form of conversation he might preach to this human soul, as Christ did to the woman of Samaria. The missionary may have travelled fifty miles to get this opportunity, and when he goes away in the morning he wants to leave behind light and peace, as every one of God's messengers should. Such work as this is not well done by an apprentice hand in the ministry; it requires an experienced workman, and one that ' needeth not to be ashamed.'

Another most necessary quality of the travelling missionary is the power to bear solitude and isolation. He may have to ride fifty miles and not see a soul, and even at night may have to ' camp' under the trees, all by himself, with his horse as his only companion. All by himself he collects the wood for the fire, gets water for the tea, lays his buffalo robe under the shade of his buck-board, and through the night listens for his horse-bell; no human face near, and no human hand in any emergency to give assistance. And when he arrives back home, especially if there is no parsonage, but only a small hut where his few books are kept,—and these often disfigured and injured by the mice which have taken possession during his absence,—the missionary need be no coward. The more apostolic faith he has, the more comfortable he will be in his solitary surroundings. When we realize these things, and the self-denial that is necessary in order to continue such a life year by year, is it any wonder that so few clergymen can be found who will undertake it, and that those who do soon find the life unbearable? Not one young man in a hundred is able to endure it long. Often these men return to England from the Colonies, to be looked upon as deserters from the mission field; but let those who blame them try their experiment for a few years, and I venture to affirm that the criticism will be much moderated, and sympathy with this form of missionary enterprise will be more abundant.

In connection with this aspect of Colonial missionary work, I will tell a few simple stories of my Muskoka experience. I began the Rosseau Mission, and built the church there at the head of those beautiful lakes. In the middle of the summer we had crowds of visitors from all parts of Canada and the States, and some even from Europe, who filled the large hotel, and made good congregations on the Sunday; but when they went away I had similar work to that which I have pictured as being done in the North-West. In those days few of the settlers had accommodation for a horse, and therefore the travelling had to be on foot. Sometimes the settlers would be as much as twelve miles apart, and the so-called roads were merely a blaze through the woods. Therefore, to go from point to point on foot in the short winter days was not always easy, and if one got benighted he might suffer inconvenience, and fail even to reach any covering. This several times happened to me, and I had to spend the night in the woods all alone. On one occasion I had reached a distant lumber shanty on the Friday evening, and purposed the next day to go to another shanty to hold services on the Sunday, at a place where no service had previously been held; and I sent the people word beforehand to expect me. The place was in the woods some twelve miles off as the crow flies, and I hoped to find some mode of communication between the shanties, and so to be taken safely to my destination. However, on that morning there was no connection, and the road that was used was nineteen miles round; but the master of the shanty offered to go two or three miles with me, and show me an abandoned trail, by which I could reach the place of service in a journey of only nine miles. I started in early morning with my guide, and having left him, I pressed on over fallen trees through the snow, quite confident that I should accomplish the object of my journey.

By-and-by I reached the 'Skid roads,' where logs had been cut and piled, and the walking was very easy and pleasant. Now I was elate, and expected soon to hear human voices and to see human faces; and going straight on, it seemed that I could not miss my way, when lo! at the end of the road there were impenetrable woods.

Another road was tried, and at the end again the woods appeared; and still another, with the same result. No men were about, and snow had fallen to hide their tracks. The more I tried to find my way through these roads, which were so much alike, the worse it seemed, and I failed altogether. But what was I to do? The sun had gone down, and the last twilight was departing. Several times I had passed a pile of logs, and noticed some in the centre were shorter than the others, so that I could just get inside and secure a little protection. On arriving there, the thought came to me that I must break my trail, as there were wolves in these woods; so, several feet off, I threw my overcoat down and jumped on it, and next my surplice, and then at the pile of logs, pulled them all inside after me, and there I remained during the long cold January night.

The snow glittered like silver in the moonlight, the silence was intense; now and then it was made more evident by the cracking of the trees by the frost. The call of the night owl made the scene weird and almost unearthly, and about one o'clock in the morning I heard the pattering of many feet, which were coming nearer and nearer to my shelter. It was a pack of wood wolves, who were on my footsteps, and hunted perhaps for an hour over the path where I had walked. As they came near to the logs they sniffed, and followed the trail again, going up and down until they were tired, and then left me to solitude, if not to peace. By the protection of God I was saved from destruction that night, because I, by what seemed an accident, broke the trail from the scent of those hungry wolves.

In the morning I tried again to find the right road through, but quite failed, and returned to the former shanty late on the Sunday evening, wholly worn out, but in time to hold service with a lot of wild rough Irishmen and Roman Catholics, who in other circumstances could not be gathered to join in the services of our Church.

While the supper was being hastily prepared these men put all sorts of questions to me as to how I had spent the night, and whether I had been near the wolves, of which they had a horror ; and when they saw me quiet and in no way excited, and not anxious to make a scene, the rough men appeared to be quite touched and full of sympathy. Never after that was any rudeness visible when I visited that lumber shanty, although I was only 'a Protestant minister.'

A few weeks after this event I found my way by another route to the shanty I had intended to visit, and fulfilled my promise. Then I learned that when I did not turn up the people were anxious to hear of my safety, for the region in those days was a very wild one between the Maganetawan River and Nipissing Lake, although now it is a well settled country.

On calling at the Rosseau Hotel one day, I met a gentlemanly man whom I had not seen before, and as he looked at me with an evident desire to make my acquaintance, I spoke to him, and found that he had settled some nine or ten miles off, on the road to the Maganetawan River. Our conversation ended by his giving me a warm invitation to visit him when I went that way, and to stay at his place whenever it was convenient for me to do so.

After a time I called, and wished to arrange for a service, as there were two or three families a mile or two away who never had that privilege. As no one was in sight, I called and called until the son appeared, and he told me that they had no proper accommodation for me, and asked me to go on to the next place, as his father was not in. However, as I was tired, I told him that his accommodation would be quite sufficient for me, and I refused to go any further that night.

After a time the father came in, and apologized for his non-appearance, and offered me the best he had. Father and son bestired themselves, and prepared me a most comfortable bed. They cooked deer meat and potatoes, and, with some bread, we had a fine supper.

This visit was the first paid to a place which afterwards became a town, and it turned out to be in every way pleasant to those concerned. On my taking farewell of my host on the Monday morning, he confessed that he saw me coming on the Saturday evening, and that he was so distressed at his want of accommodation for me, he had hidden himself among the turnips he was hoeing, and only appeared when he found that I would not go away. He promised, however, he would not do so again, and for years he never failed to give me the kindest and most hospitable welcome.

Yet another story of colonial missionary life. Twenty miles beyond the house of my friend was a small hut, perhaps twelve feet by twelve. On calling there one day to tell them of the service to be held at ' the Depôt,' three or four miles off, the old lady, a daughter of Ireland, made me promise that the next time I came that way I would return with them and stay for the night; 'for indeed the good Lord would bless their shanty if a clergyman once stayed with them.'

When the time came I left very comfortable quarters, and walked several miles with the family, in order to fulfil my promise. We had some tea, without milk or sugar, some bread, and I think some butter with it. After a time we had prayers, and, as I saw no preparation for bed, I began to lay my rough overcoat down on the floor, with my folded surplice for a pillow. But this the old lady would not allow. There were two beds in the small apart-ment, and there were four persons present to occupy them. I was appointed to share one of them. The old lady, with a grown-up grandson, in the simplest manner turned into the other bed, and presently the son came to share mine.

An hour had passed, and a noise was heard out-side which woke up the whole establishment. Another son had arrived with his oxen from Rosseau, where he had been on his errands for the family. The first thing he did was to inquire whether the minister had come. Then he expressed his satisfac-tion, and came also into the bed, gently pressing his brother lest he should inconvenience me; but the bed was not large enough for three, and the sides were made of round poles, which were not flattened in any way, but were just as they came from the woods, and it was my fortune to be pushed on to the round pole, with nothing between me and the wall. That was the way in which I rested that night, the people being quite unconscious of my position and discomfort. In the morning my truthfulness was sorely taxed when the anxious inquiry was made whether I had passed a good night.

Once I went down the lakes from Rosseau to Port Carling, to make a visit to the Musquosh, and found it difficult to get across a part of Muskoka Lake; at last, in a shop, I found a Scotch Highlander who offered to take me to his house for the night, and on the morrow he would in his canoe land me where I desired to be put ashore. The man had a little daughter with him, and he was partly intoxicated; yet, as I had duties pressing, I thankfully accepted his kindness. Our canoe was a very light one, and the winds became rough and the lake boisterous; the night had fallen, and we could only see the gleaming of the waters around the very top of the canoe. If one of us had moved one inch it seemed impossible that the boat could have lived in the waters—she must have gone down. The man saw the danger, and with skill broke the force of the waves, only saying sometimes, 'Steady, steady; don't move!' By a miracle we crossed safely the three miles of lake. Seldom have I felt nearer the other world than on that stormy night on Lake Muskoka.

As I stayed a day or two longer than I expected, on my return I found my friends at Rosseau organizing a party to search for my body; for the report had gone up the lakes that we were all certainly drowned. The work at Rosseau was much the same as the work in the North-West, so far as it was a mission to settlers; and a narration of these occurrences may show the real self-denying toil that is demanded of the missionary in the first stages of colonial settlement: it calls out a courage and endurance that are equal to that demanded by any other work in the world.

In this North-West only an Indian would be allowed to travel alone. Hudson Bay employés and mounted police go from station to station in small parties. Dwelling-places are found for the men, and some kind of rations are provided as a matter of course; but the missionary has to travel alone, on the ground of expense; he must find his own 'shack,' and do innumerable things which other men would regard as hardships. Whether this is good policy or not I leave to the good sense of those who have authority in the Church.

CHAPTER XIX.

CRITICISM OF CHURCH METHODS.

AT the present time the most important question for the Canadian Church to settle is the best method of work for this general mission to settlers. The Church is undoubtedly very weak in all our dioceses, even the oldest, in remote country districts. Often for many miles our Church has no stations, or, indeed, any existence whatever. Should Church-people settle in such districts, they are left to the various sects, who are more widespread and zealous than ourselves. Hence thousands of English Church-people are lost to our communion, and their children know the Church as a mere tradition in which they have no interest. These things are notorious in all our dioceses, and spasmodic efforts are made to recover lost ground; but why should not the failure be allowed, and new means be tried to meet the fresh conditions of our colonies in these extensive countries? For many years now it has been evident that we have neither the men nor the means to cope with the difficulties of large,

sparsely-settled districts.   At present we shut our
eyes to the fact, by making a so-called 'mission'
cover fifty or a hundred or two hundred miles, and
supply it with a solitary priest, or deacon, or lay-
reader, and even such missions are often vacant, or
cannot be supplied continuously. The missioner's
health breaks down, or the solitude oppresses him,
or the apathy of the few who belong to the Church
discourages him, or the zealous sects around under-
mine his work, or his inexperience leads him into
difficulties which he is unable to overcome, or his
sanguine hopefulness at starting leads him to make
glowing reports which cannot be sustained, and the
Church authorities are disappointed because he
cannot do impossibilities, and tell him so.

This is the usual course of such missions, and they
fail, as might be expected; for how can any man
cover a hundred miles of country, where the people
live at least a mile apart, and because of their
excessive labour are often too tired to travel on the
Sunday, or too indifferent to make any effort to do
so?   How are families to be gathered, and children
to be instructed, in all weathers, when they are not
near the small centres, which are but few and far
between, and when these are already occupied by
innumerable sects?

As one of the conditions of such work is that it
must be based on voluntary offerings, how are these
to be collected? and who is to collect them, and
when?   People in such missions have but little
money, and this only at certain times.   The

labour of collecting from them is often labour in
vain. And if the missionary would take gifts in
kind, what would he be able to do with them? He
is supposed to be usually travelling about, and the
markets are afar off, even if there be any. Then,
what is to become of the studies of such a missionary?
Where can he get books? How can he use them to
advantage if he have them? What is to become of
his own spiritual life? and how is the spirit to be
replenished out of which he has to draw the living
waters of the Gospel for others? He has no com-
panionship, no brotherly counsel, no church privi-
leges—only a monotony of life, which is repeated,
year in, year out, until brain and heart are weary,
and sometimes both moral and physical consequences ensue which are sad to contemplate.

The question arises, Can this be the right system
for such work? The plan is to take a young man,
either trained or untrained, perhaps before he is
even ordained, and to send him into a district,
promise him a certain stipend, which the people are
to supplement, and then he has to find his own way,
and to do the best he can. Any guidance given
him is usually of the slightest kind, and, by reason
of the distance from the source of authority, it may
mislead, rather than assist, the inexperienced missionary. There must be some better system than
this which would make our mission in sparse settlements more generally successful. As usual, in this
as in other matters, it comes true that 'There is no
new thing under the sun.' England and the Conti-

nent of Europe were evangelized by companies of men who worked together, each man doing his own special work for the good of the whole.

These men were called by different names, and their methods of work were not always the same; but they managed to cover the countries which they occupied with effective agencies, and with churches for Christian worship. They founded and built up the best civilizations that the world has ever seen. Their system was both a human and a divine one, and it had deep and wide foundations, and we shall have to return to it if we would build up a national faith in our colonies. Our present methods are individualistic, and rest too much on monetary considerations, and the matters which hang around them. We want men of genius, for originating methods of work adapted to special circumstances and places, as the Archbishop of Canterbury told the Society for the Propagation of the Gospel at its annual meeting two years ago. In such work hard and fast lines cannot always be laid down and followed everywhere, until they become commonplace and rigid customs, which are too antique, in a bad sense, for the work.

The condition of the Algoma, and several other of our dioceses where the work is ministering to settlers, must be taken into account if we would question the perfectibility of our present plans, and seek for others that are more likely to succeed. It will take generations to make the missions self-supporting, and many never will be such without endowments, or the provision of some extra means of support when the present grants are withdrawn.

In the meantime, what will become of the most devoted missionaries, who are broken down in health and spirits, and who in most cases will have nothing to retire upon, and for whom no other work will be offering by which they can earn a living? Their prospects are really gloomy indeed. Often I have wished, when I have heard bishops and others blaming the poor clergymen for not raising sufficient funds under such conditions, that I had the power to distribute more equally the funds of the dioceses among the men who were bravely struggling with these difficulties; and I would leave dignitaries to their own reward, and to the voluntary principle that is so earnestly forced on others. I would first of all see the distant settlements well supplied with men and means, and so lay a foundation on which a grand superstructure could be reared. Bishops and other dignitaries are more like the angels, and nearer to heaven, than the common clergy can expect to be, and hence they are more fit—if that were necessary —to live on manna than the poor missionaries who are of coarser mould, and who require bread and meat and warm clothing in the winter-time. I think this would be the general sentiment of the English people, who mostly send us their benevolences. Let the lowliest be first served, for of such is the kingdom of Heaven.

I wish we could return to the most ancient forms of missionary enterprise, and let our dioceses be

smaller and more manageable.   Let our bishops be
bishops, and not prelates.   Let the dignity be in
the work, and not in the style of living.   Simple
grace will adorn any sphere ; simple wisdom will
crown any work ; and the Master has shown how
beautiful the manger may become ; how sublime the
Cross ; how charming before the ages can be the
fishers' boat ; and the hillside where the Divine
Presence is.   And, although wealth can be consecrated to God's glory, it may be ours, in our new
conditions, to tread in the footsteps of the Redeemer,
and take up our cross and deny ourselves for Him,
and by living in His spirit show our true apostolic
succession to the world in these modern days.   If a
priest can live on a hundred pounds or a hundred
and fifty a year, collect part of it, and travel at his
own cost, let a bishop have his three hundred pounds
and be content, and keep strictly in his sphere, and
—at least, in the colonies—leave worldly dignity
alone.   He will be more respected in his office if
he be fit for it, and he will be more in touch with
his people, who often care but little for old-world
dignities and titles.

   With this simpler diocesan organization I would
seldom plant a single man down in his loneliness in
a wide district of country ; I would have small communities of clergy, under an experienced priest, who
should superintend the work of the whole district,
and be a father in God to the men who were around
him, giving them counsel, and encouragement, and
protection, and spiritual help, and intellectual

training. He would be a practical rural dean where he is most wanted. In this way freshness and vigour could be thrown into the work, and efficiency and economy would be secured. This would be a real missionary organization ; not necessarily interfering with settled pastorates, but supplementing them in some cases, and in others preparing for them when the population became more dense.

Such spots might, as of old, become religious houses and centres of light and blessing, where prayer could be offered and work could be done for the glory of God, until in many places of our vast solitudes the wilderness would rejoice and blossom as the rose. Closely connected with this subject of the methods of work adapted to our colonial Church conditions is that of the kind of bishops required, and the manner of their appointment. What has a little surprised me is the apparent want of delicacy that I have seen in the newspapers as soon as a vacancy has arisen in our North-West dioceses. Name after name is mentioned, as if a clergyman were a politician looking for office.

Considering the professed sanctity of the bishop's office, ought not ambition here to be stilled, and when the responsibility and the difficulties of the position are realized, ought not the feeling to be, ' Who is sufficient for these things'? Remembering, too, the mother Church at home, and our indebtedness to her in the past, and our dependence upon her help in the future, it does seem out of place to raise the question of our independence of the Church

authorities at home in the selection and appointment of bishops for our vacant dioceses, especially
in the far West.   English Churchmen, above all
men, might well realize what is meant by their belief
in the communion of saints, and be thankful when
England, in our need, gives us of her best, not only
of her money, but of her cultivated sons, who are
incomparably the richest gifts she can offer to her
Colonies.

Men of the world know, without any dispute, the
advantages of a European education for prominent
offices anywhere; and, while England is willing to
open the way to colonists of great ability at home,
so as practically to make the Empire one, and
England to be wherever the Union Jack waves, it is
surely ungracious to raise the question in the Church
—of Canada for the Canadians—when bishops are
required whose dioceses cannot exist without the
benevolences of the motherland.   Surely the best
and most worthy men should be appointed as bishops
wherever they may be found.   Hence I cannot
look with the highest satisfaction upon the changes
lately brought about in the Church of England
in Canada.   Not that a general synod of the whole
Church can be greatly objected to, if it be required
—and Methodists and Presbyterian organizations
already have their general conferences and assemblies
—but the assumption of conferring new titles without the formal sanction of ecclesiastical authorities
in England is surely not ancient, but very modern
Church order, and in history it will stand out as a

departure from old customs, which will not add such dignity to the Archbishoprics of Canada as they would have worn if, at the next assembly of English Church Bishops gathered from all parts of the world, His Grace of Canterbury conferred such titles, with the sanction and authority of the whole English Church.

CHAPTER XX.

THE SASKATCHEWAN COUNTRY.

THE Earl of Southesk, who travelled in the North-West years ago, speaks of the country as the 'pleasant Saskatchewan country.' No description could be more apt, until you arrive at the mountains, when of course the scenery is magnificent. From Winnipeg to Edmonton the aspect of the country for hundreds of miles has a great sameness; it is gently undulating, and studded with clumps of poplars and spruce firs, and gives the impression of peacefulness and rest, with a sense of neatness and cultivation, as if the traveller were in the outlying parts of an old English park, too far from the house to receive particular attention. All the scene gives a picture of pleasant freedom. The calm blue sky overarching vast distances in the daytime ; the sunrise, pompous and glorious, with rich golden colours variously mingled with the blue of the sky, gives an idea of sweet majesty ; and in the eventide the sunsets are unsurpassed for graceful splendour. In sky-scape, or

11—2

the varied scenery of the heavens, few skies in the world can surpass these, and, as nature is full of harmony, not only to the ear but also to the eye, the impression is unique and pleasant, and it is not to be wondered at that the natives of the Saskatchewan love their land, and return to it from their journeyings with gladness. Besides the vastness of the scenes above and below, on the banks of brooks and rivers, there are innumerable broken, hilly spots, filled with vegetation, generally well wooded, where poets might make homes of beauty and rest. It is as if Nature had said : ' The plains are made for agriculture, and the toil of brave hands; but I have also made spots where the thinkers of a nation may live to idealize the common life, and thus make a perfect nation.'

On ascending to the mountains, the hills are steeper, and the views are more extensive, but there is much the same vegetation. Only in some places do the Rockies show their full height, because of the gradual ascent for hundreds of miles. Yet they seldom disappoint the beholder. When the sun is shining, and the mists are lifted to reveal God's splendour, they entrance the attention, and charm the mind to reflection on the awful silent forces which of old placed them there, and now seem to guard them continually, by night and day, by summer and winter, through long ages as men reckon time, saying to every mood of the human spirit, ' One day is with the Lord as a thousand years, and a thousand years as one day.' The name of the mountains rather jars upon the mind, and the inexperienced traveller might expect to see a bare and almost repulsive scene when he beholds them. The 'Rockies,' however, are as beautiful as any of the great mountain ranges which the world possesses—certainly as seen from a distance. The impression they make is that of graceful majesty. I can imagine the mountains of India as being more gorgeous in the lower scenery, but not as of a majesty more graceful in the higher regions.

The far West country has hill and dale, gentle brooks, flowing rivers, broad plains, and magnificent mountains; and these indicate great natural advantages, and almost illimitable possibilities for that portion of mankind which may make it a home, and help on the march of human history.

The geology of our country speaks of immense changes which have been preparing an abode for man, and is in itself a prophecy of certain fulfilment. Our soil is of unexcelled richness; beneath it are almost boundless coal-beds; gold is washed down from the mountains in sufficient quantities to make a paying industry. Our wheat is equal to any grown in the world, when proper care is used in its cultivation. Around us are lakes stocked with an abundance of fish. There are indications of salt, petroleum, and kindred substances, such as naphtha, etc. Iron. probably in abundance, is evident over large distances, as I have proved, from the Eagle Hills to the Mountain Fort, and also in the Edmonton district, over a country hundreds of miles in extent.

Then, as to home-life, and the possibilities of it in the Saskatchewan, we have many advantages, with, of course, our drawbacks. We have no ants or insects which eat up our furniture and our books, as there are in Africa ; no loathsome reptiles to destroy, as in South America; we have innocent pests in our gardens and fields, such as the gopher and the mole, but what are these in a new land which only contained hunters for many ages? The climate is extreme in summer and winter; during the other parts of the year it is healthy and very pleasant, and fitted to produce and sustain a manly race. Our seasons are much the same as in England, only we are in extremes; our latitude somewhat corresponds with that of Great Britain, yet our seasons are later, because we are far to the west. Our springs are late in coming, because the nights are cold while the days are warm ; when they do come it is with a rush, as if Nature hastened to make up for lost time. Then, at the end of May, and during June, the roses bloom in wild luxuriance, and fill the air with fragrance. The saskatoon and wild cherry-trees are covered with their white blossoms, and charm the sight on all sides ; then come on, in their course, innumerable wild flowers—asters and others decking the earth everywhere with graceful loveliness. Then our autumns—who can picture them with their gaudy colours, their dreaminess, as if they were bestowing a benediction on the departing summer ; their warm days, and cool evenings, and long nights; after the work of the day the gentle firelight giving invitation to gentle friendships, and the quietude of family life ?

As yet the capabilities of our soil and climate have not been properly tested, so as to show what fruits and flowers and shrubs will thrive best in our gardens; for, as yet, out of the towns gardens are seldom made around our dwellings: the farm reaches up to the doorstep, and almost invades the house. In the country we are at present a slovenly people, and a taste for flowers is at a discount; the work is so hard and incessant for the men, and the women are so occupied with their poultry, and their cows, and their butter-making, and their housework, that they are all too much engaged to work leisurely in a garden, or even to enjoy the luxury of one. Hence, our log-houses are bare places, and their surroundings are commonplace beyond description. But although we may not manage orchards on a large scale, there seems to be no reason why, in the future, the hardy apples should not grow, as our climate is not more severe than Quebec, where the finest apples are grown with ordinary care. So with plums and some kinds of pears ; probably, also, the hardier grape-vines may ripen around our dwellings in the days to come. Anything which grows in Northern Russia ought to grow here, for the conditions are much the same as those from St. Petersburg to the Sea of Okhotsk. We have many delicious wild fruits which, with cultivation, serve for summer and winter use. Preserves are made of our wild cranberries, strawberries, gooseberries, black and red currants. The wild raspberry especially is a fine fruit, useful both in summer and in winter-time. The saskatoon is a delicious berry for summer use, and, when served with cream and sugar, makes a dessert fit for a queen. These fruits may all be had in most years for the picking, so kind is Nature to our first necessities.

Some of the people have grown the cultivated strawberry. In my garden the rhubarb plant comes to perfection, and the different red currants live, and often bear enormous crops. Potatoes, peas, beans, asparagus, cabbages, etc., and the small salads grow here as well as in any country, and the simplest home need not be without an abundance of them. A little care will grow the herbs of Europe, such as mint and thyme, but parsley must be sown year by year. Simple annual flowers remind us of the sweet cottage gardens at home, the sweet-williams flourish, and sow their seed as they have opportunity, and the pinks and carnations thrive with a little trouble. There is a hardy candytuft, with an exquisite white blossom, which is not willing to leave our gardens when we have once placed it there ; the English marigolds willingly sow themselves without any protection ; and the pansies come up and flower early in the springtime, and all through the summer.

Our many shrubs, when in flower, would grace a lawn in England, and, if trained, they would rival the hawthorn, which we have wild here, or the laurel. For years the common lilac has blossomed

with me, and once or twice the white lilac, but the
latter is always sickly, and comes to very little,
perhaps because the moles eat the roots. As for
roses, I have tried to grow them until I became very
discouraged, and I fear the labour will be in vain
unless they are newly planted year by year.

In many cases I do not blame the climate so much
as the insects and vermin for the failure in my
experiments. I planted the Canadian sugar-maple
seed, with many other tree seeds, and the maple
seed grew; but the saccharine matter attracted one
insect after another, and they ate the leaves as fast
as they could grow. I raised some fine Austrian fir-
trees from seed, and brought them on splendidly
through two winters, but in the third winter the
wild rabbits ate them all up in one night, and thus
my hopes of rearing this beautiful tree, as a magnificent ornament to our North-West, were destroyed.
In a catalogue issued by a Toronto firm of experienced nurserymen they say, in speaking of hardy
shrubs for hedges: 'The Osage orange would make
an excellent hedge, but it is too tender for the
climate around Toronto.' But I have reared here,
and still have, the Osage orange thriving as if it
were native to the soil, and it has never had protection, nor does it in the least require it. When
hedges are wanted in the North-West, this will
prove the tree for that purpose, being quick of
growth, prickly, dense ; and it can be pruned to any
extent; it is also very handsome in its foliage.
Besides the above, I expect, from present appear-

ances, to cultivate as shrubs the syringa, the privet, and the guelder rose.

As for the common clovers, they are not likely to be used much in the North-West for hay ; they flower in the garden, but are of slender growth, and soon die out ; however, the timothy, in low rich situations, makes good crops and seldom fails. With me the Bokhara clover has lived for years, and sown itself; it is able to survive our winters, and it would yield large crops several times in the summer. Farmers should give it their attention, for seedsmen recommend it, and it is certainly adapted to our North-West. It is, I have observed, also excellent for bees, which delight in its white flowers, and would make exquisite honey from them.

Some of these matters may prove useful and interesting to a large class of immigrants, and those contemplating emigration, who have the home feeling, and who, in going to another land, wish to make homes and enjoy them. With many this is a great motive in crossing the sea, and beginning life afresh ; they wish to keep their children around them, and to take with them some of the graces and refinements of civilization, and I hope I have made it evident that this, however difficult, is certainly possible.

CHAPTER XXI.

EMIGRANTS AND EMIGRATION.

FROM my experience in Muskoka, and for many years in Edmonton, I must have had the matter of emigration constantly before my mind; and yet I find it difficult to say anything *ex cathedra* on such a subject; the longer I am behind the scenes, the less positive can I be concerning the classes who should emigrate to our colonies, or, indeed, to any particular part of Canada. Our towns and cities often have openings for enterprising young men who cannot find proper employment in England. When these openings occur through the help of friends, a young and steady man should not throw away his opportunities, for new countries are not so crowded as the old ones are; but let it be remembered that, in emigrating, a man needs all the qualities by which success is won anywhere. Here the temptations are not less—perhaps they are intensified. The young man must have ability, and know how to use it; he must have a character and value it; he must choose his companions with care, and follow in all things the way that conscience dictates. Canada is no home for the indolent, the faithless, or the vicious; such persons will soon reach the lowest depths of degradation, and wish that they had stayed in England. Again, our trades are filled with men who are accustomed to the ways and ideas of a new country, and who do not follow old methods of work. If an artizan would work as hard at home as he must do out here, he might find life easier and more pleasant. What we chiefly need are men who like a country life, and are accustomed to it, and who have fair means to settle on land, and turn our rich prairies to advantage. These are welcomed, and are likely to be successful wherever they may settle. This applies to our North-West especially. Here, also, occur opportunities for the use of money, in good investments in land, and in general business, and the opening up of industries that may be lucrative to the investor, and advantageous to the country as a whole; yet these matters require great experience and caution, if speculations are not to end in disaster. In thinking of emigration, a benevolent person is concerned chiefly with the innumerable poor who, in old lands, struggle for existence, and find it difficult to live, save in a state of semi-starvation. Many of these are attached to a country life, and do not mind work when they have a motive for it; they are men with brave hearts, but they are wanting opportunities to attain a noble independence. If such men once get on their feet in the North-West, they can make homes, feed themselves and their families, and live comparatively free from carking care, and the misery of town life and its uncertainties. I have known many persons who have, from the most unpromising conditions, by the possession of such moral qualities as perseverance, honesty, and good sense, attained to comfortable positions. Our settler's life is a very simple one, and he can learn by degrees how to turn his land to account.

His first wants are a simple log-house, with only necessary furniture. Often his gun will help his larder. He gets a few acres ploughed, and a small garden planted; a cow for milk is a luxury, and is soon obtained; if he should live by a lake, or river, he manages some fish, and if he have a trade, he would find it useful, either to bring in money, or as an exchange for work on his place. His necessities press him, and keep him up to the mark. He will have great difficulties, but they will lessen year by year until they disappear altogether. Such a settler, even from the towns of England, will awaken our interest, and for a time our pity, but his case would be the same in his struggles at home, and then it would be without the chances that his toils would end in success and comfort, as they may do here. Hence, when I have observed the trials and difficulties of the poor settlers who, it may be, have come from cities, and knew nothing previously of country life, I have tried to compare their present trials with those of their friends whom they have left behind, and I have hoped that the illusions by which they were led to cross the sea, and plant themselves and their children in a new land, and in new circumstances, would ultimately issue to their great advantage. Here are certainly pure air, pure water, some wild game, land to till, wood and coal to burn, and gold to mine on the Saskatchewan, all free to the most miserable of mankind. I am thinking now of the lowest class of emigrants, who are often discouraged, and for whom one would not care to be responsible. And yet it seems so important in the present age to discourage the rush to towns and cities, and to bring men into natural relations with the land, that almost any inconvenience might be endured, by any class of people in this generation, so that the great end of the natural life might be attained in the years which are to come in the evolution of mankind.

As for making money and growing rich by the cultivation of land in the North-West, or in any other country, this motive cannot truthfully be presented to intending emigrants. Agriculture is the natural life for man, and by it men may supply their necessities and build up healthy homes. Wealth is not necessary for man, and it can be done without. The greatest nations have been greatest when their lives were simplest, and agriculture was their chief occupation. Let men emigrate, and settle on land in order to make homes, and to live healthy and natural lives, without greed, or restlessness, or insane egotisms, and then human misery can be lessened, and the world's happiness and peace may be increasingly secured. The age is pessimistic because its life is so unreal, and its aims are so illusory, and altogether so out of harmony with nature and with religion. It asks, 'Is life worth living?' The answer is, for the most part, ' *Your* life is not worth living. Return to the simple natural life of labour, and ennoble that life by industry, virtue, and intelligence, and then the world may yet be a good place for God's human children.' To any men with this view of things the North-West will give a welcome, and bestow an inheritance that is not to be had in crowded Europe, an inheritance which shall be to them and to their children's children.

Still, the class of emigrants most desirable is the farming class, who have large or small means, and who will be prudent, industrious, and persevering. The Edmonton district is equal to any other for ranching, or mixed farming, and, with the moral qualities which have been indicated above, this class is sure to prosper in our North-West.

It remains for me to mention another class of great importance who come to our North-West, viz, the sons of gentlemen, and a great many of these are the sons of clergymen and ministers of religion. During twenty years I have met with a great many of this class, until I have ceased to wonder at the numbers of young men, of good education and position, who are unable to find lucrative occupations in England. I have observed how difficult their position often is, and how seldom they answer the hopes of the friends who send them out.

It is supposed that if a young man finds his way to Canada and our North-West, he will soon obtain occupation, and become independent in life. This is a great mistake ; the trades are filled, the professions are crowded, and, as a rule, the farmers themselves do all the work they can in order to save wages. At busy seasons handy men can get employment for a time ; then, when work slackens and the winter is at hand, hired men generally are dismissed, and they have to find any accommodation that offers ; their wages are soon used up, and if they board at hotels their surroundings are full of temptations which imperil their moral characters, and hinder their success in life. Thus the men may become restless ; having tired the patience of their relatives, and used up their means, and having formed bad habits, they become useless wanderers, and lose their way in life almost beyond redemption. I do not say this of all gentlemen's sons, but it is true that very many of them become the victims of such circumstances. Suppose any of this class find employment on farms, the work is hard, the living is poor, little self-respect can be cultivated. Generally speaking, these men are in a false position, and, although they bear it bravely for a time, they become disgusted with their life and with Canada, and the best of them return home disappointed, and ready to blame the country which would gladly have adopted them permanently had their circumstances been more favourable.

When families emigrate together, the father and

mother can look after their sons, and give them direction and society; when this cannot be done, friends and relatives may be engaged for these duties. Failing all these, it would be a boon worth any reasonable expense to place young men under responsible people, who will fairly teach the methods of farming which the country requires, give the young men pleasant society, keep them in contact with their friends and relatives, and when the time comes, help them to choose land for themselves, and encourage them to settle down in the best neighbourhoods available. In this way young men might have fair chances of pleasant settlement, and hundreds guided and helped in such ways would become successful and prosperous, who otherwise must prove utter failures. How is it to be expected that youth and inexperience should make their way in new and most difficult circumstances, when even at home, surrounded by old customs and influences, these very men need such special and watchful care?

Objections are sometimes raised to this useful, and often necessary, protection for young men in our Colonies, on the ground of the abuse to which such a system for the protection of young men is liable. I venture to affirm that the misuse of any system is no valid reason against its right use. There must be many respectable men, well versed in colonial life, and well known to the clergy of our Church, who, for small compensation, would act as fathers and protectors to young men, and in that way all concerned would be benefited : the country in which such men would settle, the men who would look after them, the Church with which these young men are mostly connected, and the parents and guardians in England, who are often disappointed at the venture they have made in sending their inexperienced boys to difficulties, privations, and temptations, before which it would only be reasonable to expect them to fail.

In full view of all the drawbacks in the life of the emigrant, remembering the intense struggle for existence in the Old World, and in the cities of the civilized world everywhere, I should never discourage the immigration here of the right sort of men, especially those with families, who are naturally anxious for the settlement of their sons where costly professions are not required, and mere learning, except for personal cultivation, would be almost useless. A farmer's life can be very independent, healthy, and peaceful, and, where the family affections are strong, a noble human existence is possible ; and as for refinement, there can soon be realized the amount of it the family bring with them in themselves ; and with a little music and books, and a few well-known flowers, plain food, and sound rest at night, many a family would have no desire to return to the worry and care of city life, even if that were possible. It is true that one of the luxuries of the immigrant is the regretting of old scenes and times, when the discomfort of their former state has receded into a distant memory. The remembrance of former times at least reveals what the life might have become if the ideal of the past had been fully realized ; but this is seldom the case with any of us. Our wishes are in extremes : when we might enjoy something that we have we yearn for the opposite, which perhaps before we were tired of and sought eagerly to change. Hence the murmuring of educated settlers amounts to little ; it is a requiem of regret and affection to the old days, however sad and troubled they really were, which are now no more ; and any expression of such regret should be appraised at its proper value.

CHAPTER XXII.

THE FUTURE OF NORTH-WEST CANADA.

OUR Eastern Indians, and certain people in Europe, have spoken of our Saskatchewan and Western Countries as the ' Land of the Setting Sun.' It is an indefinite description, but not more indefinite than is the country itself. A few years ago these new lands were known to only a few persons, and if they returned to Europe, or the eastern parts of Canada, they were regarded as great travellers ; but now that the Canadian Pacific Railway so quickly carries its human freight, these regions are found to be the world's great natural highway to the East. This has been the instinct of travellers for three hundred years.

Columbus conceived that he, on coming West, had reached the East ; hence his mistake as to the size of the world helped his enterprise, and gave the name of Indians to the natives, who might well have been called Asiatics.

So with later travellers : they have sought persistently for a north-west passage to Asia from

Europe, and they have found that passage by the railway which has opened up these regions, and closely connected them with the far East. We are now at the doors of ancient and vast empires, such as China and Japan, and these nations must influence greatly our destiny in these border countries. Nature seems to have made our extensive plains, and our coal-fields, and our splendid soil, to be the stay of great peoples, who in the future will traffic with the East, giving it their produce, and receiving theirs in return.

Placing us thus on one of the world's central highways necessarily involves additions to our population, and to our wealth, which will surprise the future generations. The twentieth century may see these North-West regions the very centre of the world, with cities on the Columbian coast as great and magnificent as old Tyre and Carthage were, and inland towns as great and prosperous as Birmingham or Manchester.

North-West Canada has all these promises if the old British stock, and the old British virtue, rule in the land. Our climate will rear the highest possible race of mankind physically, if the mental, moral, and spiritual qualities are carefully cultivated with the physical, in order to make a well-balanced and perfect nation. Humanity here may be worthy of the past ages, and the great inheritances of which we take possession.

Rumours are rife already of railways connecting Northern British Columbia with Hudson Bay, thereby shortening by a thousand miles the route to Great Britain, and thus opening up for the Saskatchewan country the world's markets, both in Europe and Asia.

Also it has been found practicable, by Behring's Straits, to connect us with the great Siberian and Russian railways, and this will work wonders on our position in relation to the world, and will cause changes too boundless for the imagination to adequately picture. Twenty-five years more will turn some of these possibilities into facts.

Does Canada realize the vast import of these impending events, on which her very life and destiny hang? What does it mean? Russia, the most ambitious of the nations, will be close at our doors, and able at her will to pour her disciplined hordes—the very hordes, as I believe, that troubled and overran the Old World for centuries, and nearly conquered Europe—those hordes of Mongols and Tartars, scientifically trained, and relying on the tremendous forces which science has in late years placed at the disposal of great armies. She will be on the North Pacific, as she is on the North Sea in Europe, ready for attack on civilization, but defended herself by her impregnable barriers of snow and ice—in days to come the pirate of the nations, and the enemy of freedom everywhere.

Yes, Canada! This ambitious and perfidious Russia will soon be at our gates with her millions of bayonets, her tremendous forces, her innumerable Cossacks and Tartars, led by the most unprincipled and astute intellects the world has seen. These will find us open to attack, as soon as our prosperity lures their greed, their lust, and their ambition. Why has Russia impoverished her finances to build her railroads, and why does she keep a vast and powerful fleet in the North Pacific? Only for purposes of conquest, and in order that her ambition may have free play, and that she may use her opportunities. Do Canadians who talk of independence fully consider what they do? And do they know how helpless they are apart from the mother country if great emergencies should arise? These emergencies may seem yet a long way off, but in the life of nations they really are close at hand.

How fortunate for Canada is the fact that Alaska belongs to the United States, and not to ourselves! The United States, whose sympathy with Russia has been often manifest, may in a century, or even less, be glad to enter into an alliance with Canada, and the common motherland, when Russia is predominant in the North Pacific, for the protection of our freedom, our honour, our civilization, and our very existence as independent nations.

Besides events connected with Russia, we people of North-West America, as a part of the British Empire, may be greatly influenced by the England of the East—viz., the new Japanese power. Perhaps Russia may be checkmated in her designs in the far East, and find a foe close at hand equal to her diplomacy and her ambition; but even then Canada, and especially North-West Canada, will be surely drawn into the maelstrom—she cannot be indifferent. Supposing that Japan brilliantly builds and manages her fleet, and conquers China with her armies, and marshals the whole yellow race by sea and land, what would Canada—yes, what would all America—say and do? The world's greatest events in the impending years for Canada, and even for Europe, may transpire, not in Europe, or on the borders of India, but in the new, yet ancient, Pacific Seas.

THE END.

Elliot Stock, Paternoster Row, London.